SPARE PARTS

by

Elizabeth Page

SAMUEL FRENCH, INC.
45 WEST 25TH STREET   NEW YORK 10010
7623 SUNSET BOULEVARD HOLLYWOOD 90046
LONDON   TORONTO

Copyright © 1988, 1990 by Elizabeth Page

ALL RIGHTS RESERVED

CAUTION: Professionals and amateurs are hereby warned that SPARE PARTS is subject to a royalty. It is fully protected under the copyright laws of the United States of America, the British Commonwealth, including Canada, and all other countries of the Copyright Union. All rights, including professional, amateur, motion pictures, recitation, lecturing, public reading, radio broadcasting, television, and the rights of translation into foreign languages are strictly reserved. In its present form the play is dedicated to the reading public only.

The amateur live stage performance rights to SPARE PARTS are controlled exclusively by Samuel French, Inc., and royalty arrangements and licenses must be secured well in advance of presentation. PLEASE NOTE that amateur royalty fees are set upon application in accordance with your producing circumstances. When applying for a royalty quotation and license please give us the number of performances intended, dates of production, your seating capacity and admission fee. Royalties are payable one week before the opening performance of the play to Samuel French, Inc., at 45 W. 25th Street, New York, NY 10010; or at 7623 Sunset Blvd., Hollywood, CA 90046, or to Samuel French (Canada), Ltd., 80 Richmond Street East, Toronto, Ontario, Canada M5C 1P1.

Royalty of the required amount must be paid whether the play is presented for charity or gain and whether or not admission is charged.

Stock royalty quoted on application to Samuel French, Inc.

For all other rights than those stipulated above, apply to The Tantleff Office, 375 Greenwich Street, Ste. 700, New York, NY 10013.

Particular emphasis is laid on the question of amateur or professional readings, permission and terms for which must be secured in writing from Samuel French, Inc.

Copying from this book in whole or in part is strictly forbidden by law, and the right of performance is not transferable.

Whenever the play is produced the following notice must appear on all programs, printing and advertising for the play: "Produced by special arrangement with Samuel French, Inc."

Due authorship credit must be given on all programs, printing and advertising for the play.

ISBN 0 573 63032 1   Printed in U.S.A.

for Robin and Genevieve

No one shall commit or authorize any act or omission by which the copyright of, or the right to copyright, this play may be impaired.

No one shall make any changes in this play for the purpose of production.

Publication of this play does not imply availability for performance. Both amateurs and professionals considering a production are *strongly* advised in their own interests to apply to Samuel French, Inc., for written permission before starting rehearsals, advertising, or booking a theatre.

No part of this book may be reproduced, stored in a retrieval system, or transmitted in any form, by any means, now known or yet to be invented, including mechanical, electronic, photocopying, recording, videotaping, or otherwise, without the prior written permission of the publisher.

IMPORTANT BILLING AND CREDIT REQUIREMENTS

All producers of SPARE PARTS *must* give credit to the Author of the Play in all programs distributed in connection with performances of the Play and in all instances in which the title of the Play appears for purposes of advertising, publicizing or otherwise exploiting the Play and/or a production. The name of the Author *must* also appear on a separate line, on which no other name appears, immediately following the title, and *must* appear in size of type not less than fifty percent the size of the title type.

All producers must also show the following credit in all programs:

> "Originally produced Off-Broadway at
> Circle in The Square Downtown."

Spare Parts was produced at Circle in the Square by Pamela Kantor in association with Douglas L. Feldman and Paul A. Kaplan, under the direction of Susan Einhorn, with scenery by Ursula Belden, costumes by Elsa Ward, lighting by Norman Coates, and stage management by Crystal Huntington, with the following cast:
(in order of appearance)

HENRY	Stephen Hamilton
LOIS	Robin Groves
JAX	Donna Haley
SELMA	Margo Skinner
PERRY	Reed Birney

Characters

LOIS — Mid-to-late thirties. She works as a gardener in a greenhouse. Yet for all her mucking about in the mud, she's a spiritual creature filled with wild fairy tale fantasies about life. She's full of contrasts: she's earthy and mercurial, intelligent and obtuse, selfish and compassionate. She has an upper middle class background and an ivy league degree, yet cares little for money or special distinctions. Heterosexual her whole life, she's now in love and living with a woman. Pretty, with an off-beat sense of humor, she attracts people who vie to protect her.

JAX — Mid-to-late thirties. A lesbian and Lois' girlfriend. She came up the hard way—her blue collar father deserted her mother early on and she spent her childhood in other people's houses. She put herself through community college and works in a women's bar. She has all the trappings of a hard climb—she's tough, sarcastic, defensive and smart. She's also tender and vulnerable—a side she hides from everyone but Lois, who sees through her quick temper. Funny, sexy and extremely attractive, she's the hot spot in a room—if she wants to be.

SELMA   Early forties. Lois' upstairs neighbor and former roommate. If she got along with her parents, she'd be wealthy. As it is, she's very comfortable and works full-time as a volunteer in an AIDS clinic. A class-conscious liberal, she'd never send a child to public school. Divorced and childless, she's determined to be a constant in Lois' life. Warm, funny, pushy, and usually right.

HENRY   Twenty-nine—but looks younger. Lois' suitor and the father of her child. A clerk in a used book store—one of those fellows who graduated from college but never made it into life. Naive, tenacious, big-hearted and endearing. He's caught in the political transition: he's a man who'll vacuum and make shrimp salad but who believes women are women and men are men—or at least they ought to be. Often on overdrive, his brain moves faster than his mouth which runs a close second.

PERRY   Thirty-nine. Selma's roommate and Lois' confidant. Estranged from his upper crust parents, he's an art teacher in an elementary school. Extremely private, his homosexuality isn't apparent—especially since his romantic perfectionism has cut him off from love and made him a loner. Highly intelligent, gentle and sensitive, he's the kind of man you tell a secret. Socially poised, he's handsome, with beautiful manners and a dry wit.

Time and Place

The play takes place in the present in Hartford, Connecticut with one scene on the New Haven Green. It's episodic—divided into twelve scenes in two acts—and spans nine months from mid-December to early September.

The action takes place in seven different locations. While there are certain practical requirements, e.g. working doors, kitchen paraphernalia etc., a "realistic," physically detailed treatment is not recommended. A unit, modular set designed to depict these seven locations is ideal.

ACT I

Scene 1	Motel room, mid-December
Scene 2	Jax and Lois' apartment, late February
Scene 3	Jax and Lois' apartment, late March
Scene 4	Perry's studio, late April
Scene 5	Selma's apartment, late May
Scene 6	Jax and Lois' apartment, Fourth of July

ACT II

Scene 1	Jax and Lois' apartment, the next morning
Scene 2	Jax and Lois' apartment, three weeks later
Scene 3	Henry's bookstore, the following afternoon
Scene 4	Jax and Lois' apartment, a few hours later
Scene 5	The New Haven Green, late August
Scene 6	Hospital, hours later

ACT I

Scene 1

Motel room, mid-December. In the black. The SOUND of a MAN panting in time to his thrusts. HE cries out and then breathes deeply, exhausted, for a moment. HE becomes quiet.

HENRY. You want me to, y'know, go down on you?
LOIS. (*Too fast.*) *No*... No, thank you.
HENRY. Was it... Are you ok?
LOIS. I just need to move my legs...
HENRY. Sorry.

(*SOUND of THEM shifting in the bed. LOIS turns on the bedside lamp. THEY should appear naked but be effectively draped with sheets and blankets. LOIS has her knees up—this is a preventive measure to insure that the sperm doesn't spill out prematurely.*)

HENRY. All the girls on the swim team had hair like you. I used to think it was the chlorine. Made it slippery. Gleaming...Do you swim?... Do you swim?
LOIS. Yes.
HENRY. At a pool? (*HE licks her shoulder.*) Freshwater. A little salt. I'd like to see you in a bathing suit, standing in the water, looking out at nothing.
LOIS. Why?
HENRY. You'd be yourself. (*Pause.*) That isn't me. McGonnigal's. I go there twice a year at finals. They still card me. "Didja pass, kid?" I'm 29. Going on 30.
LOIS. Then why do you go there!

(*Pause.*)

HENRY. It's not that I go there. I just haven't stopped going there. (*Pause.*) You have the cleanest eyes.

(*SHE laughs.*)

HENRY. You do. Most women have all this black stuff... You can't see them. (*HE kisses her eyes singing...*) "He knows when you are sleeping. He knows when you're awake. He knows when you've been good or bad so... so... so...
LOIS. Be good for goodness sake.
HENRY. Do you still make a list? I do. In my heart. Head, I mean... I want to give you something, anything you want, wrap it... I like you... Anyway. Something happens, I've noticed it, when the touching part stops. (*HE takes her foot, pulls it into his lap, rubs it, rocking slightly.*) My mother used to paint her toenails. She'd walk around like a duck with a ball of cotton between each toe... You know what my favorite smell is? Old books. Libraries, deep in the stacks... That's where you'd see me. Hugging a book. (*HE curls up with his head in her lap.*) Is it all right—comfortable for you—if I sleep like this?

(*SHE strokes his hair. LIGHTS change to...*)

Scene 2

Jax and Lois' living room/kitchen, late February. There are four doors in this modest, two-bedroom, walk-up apartment: to the hall, bath and bedrooms. It's apparent that Jax and Lois have differing styles and taste, and that neither one has much money.

SELMA, *in a dripping raincoat over a nondescript suit, is standing just inside the front door.* JAX, *who's had a workout and a shower, is in the bathroom putting on her makeup and dressing up a bit for Lois' return. Pause.*

SELMA. You know what I really need? A cracker.

(*JAX enters, gets a box of Ritz for her...*)

SELMA. Ritz?

(*JAX starts to put them away ...*)

SELMA. No, no. (*Takes the box from Jax, retreats to the door.*)
JAX. You could come in.
SELMA. I don't want to drip.

(*JAX exits to the bathroom.*)

SELMA. (*Munches crackers. SHE thinks she hears someone in the hall, listens, stops listening.*) She's very late. I said Lois is very late. You don't worry? You don't worry. (*SHE munches.*)

(*At some point during Selma's next speech, JAX enters, still busy dressing and picking up. SHE's drinking seltzer from the bottle and carries a towel.*)

SELMA. It'll be fun having a new roommate. Someone to talk to. Change is good. He seems perfect—quiet, gay, neat. And polite. You can tell his mother made him stand when she entered a room. No wonder he's gay. Sorry.
JAX. When's he getting here?

SELMA. Five. Ish.
JAX. Selma, it's six o'clock.
SELMA. If he wants the room he can wait.
JAX. (*Drops her towel, exits to the hall, returns a moment later.*) He wants the room.
SELMA. He's literally here.
JAX. He's here.
SELMA. All right. (*SHE doesn't move.*)
JAX. Two suitcases.
SELMA. Men never have anything.

(*LOIS enters through the front door, dripping wet. SHE's dressed in a sou'wester, slicker, boots, coveralls and sweatshirt. SHE's holding out a hailstone which, as SHE talks, SHE takes to the kitchen, puts in a Tupperware container and stows in the freezer. As SHE continues, JAX helps her off with her rain gear and boots, putting them away.*)

LOIS. Look at this! Hi, Sel. Look, it's a miracle! Something this solid falling from the sky! It's as big as a golf ball. Once when I was little we were coming home from piano lessons and there was this pitter patter like someone had thrown a handful of sand against the windshield and my mother said, "Listen, that's hail," but I never actually saw anything. But this afternoon—you must have heard it. About four o'clock? We were in the greenhouse staking orchids and suddenly it was like war— these stones came crashing through the glass, lightning everywhere, ice shattering on the tiles. For a second, just a second, I thought, I'm dying, we're all dying, they pushed the button. But then I realized it was just nature. (*Hugging Jax.*) I hope I die with you. With you there, I mean.
JAX. (*Kissing her.*) Deal.
SELMA. You are so morbid.
LOIS. Aw... Little Left Out. (*Going to Hug Selma.*)
SELMA. I'm all wet.

LOIS. You're dry.
SELMA. Wonderful. (*SHE picks up Jax's open bottle of seltzer and splashes it on herself. Pause.*) I don't want to live with someone I don't even know, is that so terrible?
JAX/LOIS. No.
SELMA. All right then.
JAX. Give me your keys.
SELMA. Why.
JAX. So I can let him in.
LOIS. He's here?
SELMA. No sane person would still be here.
JAX. C'mon. I'll tell him you called.

(*SELMA gives Jax her keys.*)

JAX. And that you eat in bed. (*As JAX exits...*)
SELMA. If you say one...
LOIS. She won't.

(*LOIS hands her Jax's towel. SELMA doesn't dry herself, instead drying the floor where she'd spilled seltzer.*)

LOIS. You hate living alone.
SELMA. Only when I'm doing it.
LOIS. Sel.
SELMA. How're you supposed to take off your clothes when someone you don't even know is in the next room? How can you sleep. They're like magnets, strangers. You can't help yourself. And then you're holding your breath, listening, while he looks out your windows, makes up his mind... It's so awkward. He's in the bathroom. Then you're in the bathroom. Only he forgot something so when you come out he's standing there waiting.
LOIS. You have to give him back his money. Right now before he gets in.
SELMA. He'll think I'm crazy.

LOIS. You want to hold your breath the rest of your life?

SELMA. He's not going to live with me the rest of my life. You think he's going to live with me the rest of my life?

LOIS. No.

SELMA. I could get married again. If I wanted to. I could go gay.

LOIS. You're not going to go gay.

SELMA. Some people do.

LOIS. Some people just love someone.

(As LOIS gives Selma an affectionate embrace, JAX enters with PERRY in tow. PERRY carries his raincoat and is still dressed in his teaching clothes.)

JAX. *(Holding up Selma's keys.)* Your car keys.

SELMA. I'm so sorry. I just, just this second, didn't I, got here. It's pouring. Sleeting. I'm dripping, you see? Just wringing wet and I thought I'd dry off...

PERRY. The facilities...?

JAX. *(Pointing the way to the bathroom.)* Right there.

PERRY. Excuse me. *(HE exits into the bathroom.)*

SELMA. You're a dead woman.

JAX. The man had to pee.

SELMA. So he couldn't wait three seconds for you to come down and look for the right key?

JAX. He'd been waiting an hour.

LOIS. *(Bursts out laughing.)* I thought you were just having an anxiety attack. With the seltzer. Never mind.

SELMA. Lucky I'm wet. That's all I can say.

JAX. Are you wet? Selma, are you wet?

(As JAX mists Selma with the plant mister, PERRY enters. His hands are wet.)

SELMA. Will you stop!

(*THEY notice Perry.*)

    LOIS. As you can see, we're old friends.
    PERRY. There weren't any...
    LOIS. Oh. Sorry.

(*SHE offers him the towel. HE takes it but sees Selma dripping and offers it to her.*)

    SELMA. No, please.
    JAX. It's wonderful for the complexion. Water. In fact Selma makes a practice of bathing almost every day.
    LOIS. I'm Lois.
    PERRY. Perry. It's a pleasure to meet you. (*HE extends a dry hand to LOIS and THEY shake. HE hands her the towel.*) Thank you.
    SELMA. Of course you'll have your own towels upstairs.
    PERRY. I have my own towels with me.
    SELMA. Fine.

(*Pause. SELMA and PERRY start toward the door followed by a gracious LOIS and JAX, but SELMA, avoiding the inevitable, veers off and sits. Pause.*)

    LOIS. It's a beautiful room. And Selma's a wonderful roommate. We lived together for about a year until this place opened up, didn't we? Get her to make you her French toast and real cocoa some snowy Sunday.
    SELMA. Perry's an artist. He does the most marvelous things.
    PERRY. Really, I teach art classes at an elementary school. (*Short pause.*) I do some things, occasionally, on my own, after school but...
    LOIS. I'd love to see them sometime.

SELMA. Oh, I've got it. No, this is perfect. We'll do an exhibit, *yes!* At the clinic. All those blank walls.
PERRY. I don't have enough finished, I couldn't possibly...
SELMA. I *love* children's art. It's so naive.
PERRY. Oh.
SELMA. Children are naturally brilliant. Lois is pregnant.
JAX. Oh, for god's sake.
SELMA. If he's going to be living here we shouldn't have any secrets. Have you been tested?
PERRY. I beg your pardon?
JAX. Selma...
LOIS. Is very protective
SELMA. So we shouldn't talk about it? He should get sick before we embarrass someone?
LOIS. I don't think you should embarrass *anyone,* no.
SELMA. I'm not saying he's got AIDS. But he should be tested. They have marvelous new drugs that delay the onset. I'll arrange it. I work at a clinic that does fifty a day, for god's sake.
JAX. We'll get you a cowbell, Perry. Just promise you'll ring it whenever Selma gets within...
PERRY. (*To Lois and Jax.*) It was a pleasure meeting you both. If you'll excuse me... (*HE exits.*)

(*JAX lights a cigarette.*)

LOIS. You're welcome any time, Perry!... Selma, that was tactless and unkind.
SELMA. Where are you people from? He should be tested. Ignorance isn't bliss. Not any more. They have marvelous new drugs...
JAX. It's none of your business!
SELMA. I have to live with him.
JAX. No, he has to live with you. If he's still willing.
LOIS. There are gentler ways to get rid of someone.

SELMA. I'm not trying to get rid of him. I like him. And before I get attached... You don't have to deal with this every day. I do. I pull out their files, arrange for their funerals...

LOIS. Are you even sure he's gay?

JAX. With her track record? Selma could rent a room to Clint Eastwood and he'd come to breakfast in a kimono.

SELMA. You're very intolerant for someone with an alternate lifestyle.

(*There's a KNOCK on the door. LOIS goes to answer it.*)

LOIS. You never gave him keys.

SELMA. They've documented the effects of ambient smoke on a fetus, you know.

(*LOIS opens the door expecting Perry. HENRY stands there dripping wet and holding a dozen pink roses.*)

HENRY. Hi.

SELMA. Who's that?

HENRY. I would have called but I didn't know your last name. Isn't that funny? It didn't occur to me—you did, all the time—that night. That you'd disappear. What you must have thought when I didn't call. But it's not true. I couldn't find you. I called every florist, every nursery, every greenhouse. Finally. But it had taken, you know, weeks, with Christmas and all so I didn't want to just... Not at work. But then your phone was unlisted. Everyone's afraid. I had to go to City Housing and page through endless... Anyway. Can I come in?

SELMA. (*To Jax.*) Who is it?

JAX. I dunno.

LOIS. Selma, Perry's locked out.

SELMA. I'm going. (*SHE holds out her hand to HENRY who's still in the doorway.*) I'm Selma.

HENRY. Nice to meet you. I'm Henry. Moss. Henry Moss. Henry.
SELMA. How nice. Are you a friend of...
LOIS. Please, Selma.
SELMA. All right. You want me to bring anything down? Brandy? Oh, I forgot. (*Patting Lois' stomach.*)
LOIS. No, please. Let's call it a night.
SELMA. Oh. Are you mad at me?
LOIS. No.
JAX. Goodnight.

(*SHE hands SELMA her keys. SELMA exits.*)

HENRY. Is there something wrong with your stomach?
LOIS. No. Indigestion.
HENRY. I could come back another...
JAX. Who is this, hon?
LOIS. It's... uh. Henry Moss.
JAX. Henry Moss?
LOIS. You remember, the fellah I met at Christmas? The night you sent me to McGonnigal's?
HENRY. Maybe she didn't mention, I don't blame, I feel so, well I guess you wouldn't call it, well maybe, irresponsible but I wanted to call her, you, I meant to but we got so, *I* did, *she* was fine, believe me, perfect, drunk that night, and then somehow missed each other. I missed you. (*HE kisses her awkwardly on the cheek and hands her the roses.*)
LOIS. Would you... like a piece of pie? Apple pie. I made some yes—
JAX. No.
HENRY. I'm sorry?
JAX. It's not nice, Lois. It's a little tart, you wouldn't like it.
HENRY. Oh, I'm not really fond of pie, even if it is nice. That is, if it's tart. But thank you.
LOIS. Coffee then.

HENRY. Well, ok.
JAX. We're fresh out. Sorry.
HENRY. How about, here's an idea, we go out. For coffee and pie if you like. Or both of you. Fine.
LOIS. I'll get my coat.
JAX. (*To Lois.*) Sit down.
HENRY. (*Sits. Pause.*) I'm interrupting something, I know it.
JAX. Lois did mention you to me, she had a lovely time but well, when she didn't hear from you, she met someone else, it's serious, they're getting married, moving away.
HENRY. I knew it.
LOIS. That was unnecessary.
JAX. Was it? She didn't know how to tell you.
LOIS. I'm sorry, Henry.
HENRY. You set the date, hired the church, it's all done, I can't even, there's no chance, hope?
JAX. None.
LOIS. I'm so sorry. I truly am.
HENRY. Well, foolish.
LOIS. No, very nice.
HENRY. Thank you.
JAX. So pie is really out of the question. (*SHE hands him the roses.*)
HENRY. Of course. Right. Thank you. I'm sorry. I really did, I thought, goodbye. (*HE exits.*)

(*JAX lights a cigarette. After a long pause ...*)

LOIS. How was your day?
JAX. How was my day? My day was fine... Honey, you went to a college bar. Not for conversation. I mean I know it's been a long time but. Men, young men—he was supposed to be young, remember? Young men have certain assets, they do. If you like that sort of thing. Muscles. A little beef cake. The strut. That manly thing. That "baby,

let me lift your car." This pencil-dick looks like he got caught in a revolving door.

LOIS. He got me pregnant.

JAX. Miracles do happen. How'd he even get to you? Spill his gingerale down your back, what? I'm curious. Ask you for change so he could call his mother? He musta been a parade in bed. Don't tell me—he kept his socks on. And his bow tie. It was a Friday night, he musta had a bow tie. This is a gentleman you've brought home, Lois, I'll give you that. Roses. Does he stutter when he comes. "I'm cuh cuh cuh cuh coming!"

LOIS. It wasn't like that.

JAX. What was it like?

LOIS. It was just an act. He didn't touch me. I didn't feel him.

JAX. Lois, I'm gay. I don't know what you two did, what it meant to you. I'm the what-do-you-call-it, the exception here for you. A little day trip on a lifetime heterosexual cruise.

LOIS. I see. This isn't you being jealous, this is me having an identity crisis.

JAX. Jealous? Of that?

LOIS. You cannot make a baby without sperm.

JAX. Then what was wrong with Alex.

LOIS. He has herpes.

JAX. He does not.

LOIS. Well, he fucks around. It's dangerous. He could have anything.

JAX. And some thirty-year-old man you pick up in a bar doesn't?

LOIS. At least...

JAX. Alex would have gotten tested, he's good looking, he's bright, he was willing...

LOIS. I don't like Alex, ok? I don't trust him. I don't want him hanging around here, knowing he's the father.

JAX. You'd rather have someone we don't even know hanging around? Pining away for you...

LOIS. I tried. I went to the bar, I stood there...
JAX. All you had to do was pick out the healthiest, smartest looking kid you could find, get him drunk, take him to the motel. But no. You didn't *want* a nice clean kid, you wanted this Harry character...
LOIS. No.
JAX. Who's in love with you.
LOIS. I did not.
JAX. Then why is he standing at my door two months later, you wanna tell me that?
LOIS. He was the only one. The only one who asked me. Talked to me. They didn't want, they didn't want... (*SHE runs off to the bedroom, slams the door.*)
JAX. Oh, Christ. (*SHE goes to the door and knocks.*) Lo... Peach... Open up, come on... I'm sorry, it's just a shock, having him arrive like that, I'm sorry...Peach?

(*As SHE continues knocking, LIGHTS change to ...*)

Scene 3

Jax and Lois' apartment, late March. LOIS and JAX are dying Easter eggs. At the moment, JAX is poised to drop Lois' hailstone into a glass of tea.

JAX. Ok, you watching?

(*LOIS watches. JAX drops the hailstone.*)

JAX. One Mississippi, two Mississippi, three...
LOIS. Take it out! Take it out!
JAX. (*SHE pours the tea into another glass with a flourish and retrieves the hailstone.*) Et voila!
LOIS. Perfect.
JAX. Hey, you want birdshit in your tea...

LOIS. There's no birdshit...
JAX. I know, I was only teasing. It's Jesus' tears. Mary's. Freeze dried and sent to earth for pregnant women to keep in their freezers.

(*SHE gives LOIS the glass of tea and puts the hailstone back into its Tupperware container and into the freezer. LOIS resumes blowing the raw egg out of an eggshell through the small holes she's made at either end with a pin. JAX looks into the refrigerator.*)

JAX. Did you get milk?
LOIS. You won't leave me alone with her.
JAX. No, I won't. While you're carrying her, though, you're it.
LOIS. Meaning?
JAX. You're doing a great job. And cows can help you.
LOIS. Big, hanging down, fleshy udders you have to squeeze. It's like pus.
JAX. You are so gross.
LOIS. All right saliva. Like a great big glass of warm saliva.
JAX. She needs the calcium.

(*LOIS takes a bite out of the now empty egg shell.*)

JAX. What are you doing?
LOIS. She needs the calcium.
JAX. Spit that out. C'mon. You are so bad. (*SHE cleans the shells off LOIS' mouth.*)
LOIS. You never would have found anything at our Easter egg hunts. You would have starved.
JAX. You're right. Rinse out your mouth. That's a girl.
LOIS. I wouldn't let you starve. I'd give you all my best peanuts.
JAX. You are my best peanut....

(*THEY smile at each other for a moment.*)

JAX. We've gotta teach her to dance. And throw a frisbee. Very important. Can't let her go off to gym class feeling like a jerk. And softball. That was the one thing I was good at. I got my first glove when I was eight—my Uncle Xenaphon. She gets old enough, we get a team together, I could coach, you could... There's lots of stuff. Uniforms. Cookies. Driving here and there. Cheering.

LOIS. How many children do you expect would be allowed to play on a "mom and mom" softball team.

JAX. Why not?

LOIS. We'll see.

JAX. So you can stay home. Even when we're leading the league and she's pitching.

LOIS. I am doing my best. I'm carrying her. I'm doing everything I can. If something happens. I am not going to be a terrible mother.

JAX. Aw, c'mon. Every kid wants a terrible mother. Think of it. Bosco on your cocoa puffs, a little color tv mounted on your playpen—nothing but *Rat Patrol* all day long—teddy bears with detachable eyes. In fact. Raise your right hand. (*SHE picks up Lois' hand.*) I, mommy... C'mon.

LOIS. I, mommy.

JAX. Do solemnly swear to stunt my child's growth. To wean her on espresso and grain alcohol. To provide her with a map to the broom closet.

LOIS. We don't have a broom closet.

JAX. We'll get one. In short, to make her childhood, however brief, truly memorable.

LOIS. (*Singing.*) I love you...

JAX. No.

LOIS. (*Singing.*) A bushel and a peck...

JAX. No singing.

LOIS. (*Singing.*)
A bushel and a peck

And a hug around the neck...

(*Hugging her around the neck.*)

    JAX. Hugging is not allowed.
    LOIS. (*Singing.*)
Hug around the neck
Hug around the neck...

(*There's a KNOCK on the door.*)

    JAX. Honey, the real world might not understand this.
    LOIS. (*Singing.*)
A bushel and a peck
And I wanna get under the covers with you....
    JAX. (*Nuzzling her.*) You wanna take a nap? Hmm?

(*Another KNOCK ...*)

    LOIS. Perry said he wanted to dye eggs for his class.
    JAX. Your choice.
    LOIS. (*Smiles at her and gets up and heads to the bedroom.*) Tell him I'm asleep. (*SHE exits into the bedroom and shuts the door.*)

(*JAX opens the front door. HENRY walks past her and sits on the couch.*)

    HENRY. Tell Lois I'm here.
    JAX. She's not home.
    HENRY. She came in with that guy from upstairs at 1:30 and I know she's still here.
    JAX. What's on your mind, sport.
    HENRY. (*Calling.*) Lois!
    JAX. Bellow away, she's not here.
    HENRY. (*Getting up and heading for the door.*) Then she's upstairs.

JAX. (*Blocking the door.*) Let's keep this in the family, shall we?
HENRY. (*Hesitates.*) She didn't marry. Anyone.
JAX. Right. No, she didn't. How do you know?
HENRY. Never mind about that.
JAX. You want a beer?
HENRY. All right.
JAX. (*Getting him the beer.*) So, whatta you do for a living, Henry?
HENRY. You remembered my name.
JAX. You told it to me, didn't you?
HENRY. I work in a used book store.
JAX. Dusty work. Here y'go.
HENRY. Could I have a glass?
JAX. Absolutely. Sorry. (*SHE gets him a glass.*)
HENRY. She's pregnant.
JAX. Who?
HENRY. Lois.
JAX. I don't think so.
HENRY. She is. I saw her.
JAX. I see. When was this?
HENRY. Oh, she didn't see me. It's mine, isn't it?
JAX. Yours?
HENRY. My baby.
JAX. She isn't...
HENRY. That's why she wouldn't see me, told me she was getting married. She loves me. She didn't want to trap me.
JAX. (*Pause.*) You've been reading too many used books, Henry.
HENRY. No, I know it's true. The way she walks, each step sinking into the ground. The way she presses her hands into the small of her back.
JAX. I see.
HENRY. She's so kind. When I came in February she knew she was hurting me, her eyes were so big. She was

afraid, I could sense it and then when I watched her, suddenly I knew.

JAX. We're gay, Henry. Lois and I are lesbians.

HENRY. Look, I just want to talk to her, that's all. And I'm going to. Tell her that. (*HE starts to exit.*)

LOIS. (*Entering.*) Hello, Henry.

JAX. Let me handle this.

LOIS. It's too late for that.

HENRY. She is. She is pregnant.

LOIS. Yes, Henry, I am and...

HENRY. It's mine. Isn't it.

LOIS. Yes.

HENRY. Yes. Ok. It's mine. Ok. (*HE drops to one knee and takes her hands.*) Marry me. I'll take care of you. I'll take care of the baby.

LOIS. Henry, listen to me. I know this is a shock...

HENRY. I didn't expect it either but I'm not afraid and I won't leave you. And not just because you're carrying my child. Our child. Lois, ever since I met you... Could we have a little privacy. Please.

JAX. You've got about an inch left on this fuse, babe, I'm warning you.

LOIS. I cannot take care of you right at this moment, all right. Just let me deal with this. Henry, there's been a kind of, well, mistake. Or bad luck here.

HENRY. That night—birth control—who was thinking. You stepped out of the tub, you didn't want a towel... I don't mean to be rude but I can't have this kind of conversation in front of a stranger.

LOIS. Give me ten minutes. I'll call you upstairs.

JAX. No.

HENRY. We'll go to my place.

JAX. She doesn't want you. We're lovers, together, do you understand? She only did it to get pregnant. You're nothing to her, nothing to us. See. (*SHE kisses LOIS.*) Do you get it, little man, do you get it?

(*HENRY exits.*)

JAX. You don't wanna take care of me? Fine. I'll take care of myself.

LOIS. No matter what it does to me.

JAX. You want this guy? You wanna go play house with this guy?

LOIS. I wanted to explain the situation. And I don't appreciate being mauled...

JAX. He doesn't want an explanation. He wants to marry you.

LOIS. He does not.

JAX. He proposed to you, Lois, he fucking proposed to you. Down on one knee like fucking Jimmy Stewart. Fine. Marry him. Grow roses. Make babies. Just don't count on running back to me because I won't be here. (*Pause.*) I'm sorry I mauled you.

LOIS. I don't want a relationship with Henry Moss.

JAX. Then why is it so important how he feels. Why make me leave.

LOIS. Because you can't control your temper and he's a human being who deserves an explanation.

JAX. I explained it to him. Twice. We're together. We're gay. What's more to explain.

LOIS. I would have told him in a way he could understand.

JAX. Y'see, that's what I hate. A way he could understand. Because you understand each other. Because you reached an understanding when you had that incredibly understanding night together in the fucking understanding motel room. You think I like that? You think it makes me feel good?

LOIS. No, I don't. But do you think I could have managed it with someone who was callous, who just wanted to fuck me?

JAX. I don't wanna hear about it! I don't wanna think about it! I don't wanna keep seeing it in my head! Do you understand?!

LOIS. Yes, I do.

JAX. I know this was my idea. I know I deserve this. This is what happens when you want something.

LOIS. What happens.

JAX. It's falling apart and there's nothing I can do. It's the same thing, it's always the same thing. I used to run away from home when I was a kid. Then I'd get this amnesia about how horrible it was. I'd find myself wandering around, late at night, looking in my own windows, crawling back in—Fuck it! Fuck the hearth and home shit. It doesn't work.

LOIS. Then goodbye.

JAX. I wanted to be here, I wanted to stay here. I'd lie awake at night thinking about if you left. If Jimmy Stewart showed up. I thought this would fix it. This baby. That you'd stay.

LOIS. I'm right here.

JAX. For how long? It should have been me. I know it's impossible but if it was me, if we could've made her together... (*Pause.*)

LOIS. He's not so bad—as far as gene pools go, I mean. Is he?

JAX. He knows, Lois, he knows. It's all different. All of it.

LOIS. No, it...

JAX. Twice he's been here. Two times. He spent months looking for you.

LOIS. But now he knows and he's not coming back.

JAX. Says who.

LOIS. You saw his face.

JAX. Yeah. And he saw your belly.

(*LIGHTS changes to ...*)

Scene 4

Perry's studio, late April. SOUND of a DOOR being unlocked.

PERRY. (*Entering.*) Just wait, for a minute. I want to... (*PERRY turns on the light. It's a basement studio: grotto-like, private. Here, in the projects in progress and piles of supplies, is where the depth and variety of his imagination can be seen. HE stands in the midst of the studio, at a loss. No one has ever been there before except for him.*)
 LOIS. (*Off.*) Per?
 PERRY. What.
 LOIS. (*Off.*) Can I come in?
 PERRY. In a minute. (*HE doesn't move.*)
 LOIS. (*Off.*) You don't have to clean up for me, it's all right.
 PERRY. (*Not moving.*) Just a minute.
 LOIS. (*Off.*) I don't have to come in, Per. We could still make *Grand Hotel*. Perry? Let's not do this.
 PERRY. All right.
 LOIS. (*Off.*) What.
 PERRY. You can come in.
 LOIS. (*SHE comes in and stands for a moment, absorbing the atmosphere.*) It's...
 PERRY. What.
 LOIS. Safe. (*As SHE explores.*)
 PERRY. Tea?
 LOIS. Yes. Please.

(*HE fills a pot with bottled water, sets it on a hot plate and gets out mugs and sugar. HE stands, waiting for the water to boil and laughs.*)

LOIS. What?

(*HE laughs harder.*)

LOIS. You silly. It's all right.

(*HE clears his work bench and sets out cups.*)

LOIS. I think I have some biscuits. Yes.
PERRY. Well.
LOIS. It's lovely, it really is.
PERRY. No one...
LOIS. I know. (*Pause.*) He hasn't come back. I called every used bookstore in town. He either quit his job or I don't know...
PERRY. Close your eyes.
LOIS. Why?
PERRY. Because.

(*SHE does. HE brings out a marionette he's made—a whimsical cow with long eyelashes and rainbow colored spots.*)

PERRY. Open.
LOIS. Look at her!
PERRY. She needs a bell.
LOIS. She needs a microphone.
PERRY. The children like it. They each make one—it gets them using a lot of different materials, thinking—and then we put on a little show for the other classes.
LOIS. You're an artist.
PERRY. No. I just like to putter, make things. That's why... well... People expect things when you say you have a "studio."
LOIS. Can I try her?
PERRY. (*HE walks the cow over to her.*) You want to make her eat or something, just drop that finger.

LOIS. What's her name?
PERRY. (*Laughing.*) Oh dear.
LOIS. What is it? Tell me.
PERRY. Selma. But I named her before I met—I swear I did.
LOIS. (*Laughing.*) Oh dear.
PERRY. Don't tell her.
LOIS. She'd sputter but she'd love the attention.
PERRY. Please don't tell her. She doesn't even know about this place and she'd insist on...
LOIS. Oh, Perry, I'd never, no, I won't. I promise.
PERRY. I know it's silly.
LOIS. No. It's important.
PERRY. Well. (*Pouring tea.*)
LOIS. Did you ever do something really bad?
PERRY. I don't have any honey...
LOIS. Hester Prynne only did it once. Once—and a baby, a scarlet letter, she's thrown out of town. Am I terrible? Do you think I'm terrible?
PERRY. No, of course not. Besides, it was Dimmesdale...
LOIS. It was supposed to be a simple thing. Just that once. He was kind. I was frightened and he was very... We took a hot bath together. Not a shower. A bath. He rubbed my feet. Before... anything. He was very sweet and now, oh Perry, I feel, I can't explain it to Jax because she thinks I'm a traitor, it hurts her, and this baby seems like, I don't know. It all seems... (*SHE's suddenly still.*)
PERRY. What.
LOIS. (*SHE listens to herself.*) Wrong... Oh!
PERRY. Are you all right?
LOIS. It's moving.
PERRY. That's... good.
LOIS. (*Statement.*) It's alive... I didn't realize—I mean it's in there, moving around.
PERRY. Here. (*HE helps her sit.*)

LOIS. (*SHE's started to shiver.*) It's freezing. It feels like it's, Perry, it's crawling.
PERRY. (*Putting her sweater over her shoulders.*) Just relax.
LOIS. It can do what it wants, can't it.
PERRY. I'll call Jax. Or Selma. Or the midwife.
LOIS. No. Just...

(*SHE holds out her hand. HE takes it reluctantly. SHE's breathing deeply.*)

PERRY. I could get you a paper bag.
LOIS. No. (*SHE hangs onto his hand.*) I thought it would just sleep.

(*THEY sit for a moment.*)

PERRY. Better?
LOIS. What if it heard me, felt me. That I thought it was wrong. What if it was fine but now it knows that I don't—I do want it —
PERRY. I'm taking you home. (*HE lets go of her hand and moves away, starts clearing up the cups.*)
LOIS. Why did you do that?
PERRY. What?
LOIS. Leave me.
PERRY. What do you expect me to do? (*HE yells at her stomach.*) She didn't mean it, baby! She really loves you! Pretend you didn't hear it! It'll be all right!
LOIS. Stop it.
PERRY. I'm sorry. I'm sorry. It's this place. I shouldn't have people here. I wanted to show you but clearly this is not a good idea.
LOIS. Where did you live before you came to us?
PERRY. I'm taking you home.
LOIS. Where?
PERRY. In a room. In a house. With my own bath.

LOIS. But you didn't like it.
PERRY. No.
LOIS. Why not? What happened?
PERRY. Nothing. Not everyone lives from crisis to crisis. My life is even. My life is smooth.
LOIS. Why leave such perfection.
PERRY. It was too quiet. All right? Is that what you wanted to hear? I needed...
LOIS. What?
PERRY. Nothing special just... Someone to knock at the door and...
LOIS. So you could shut it. Ignore it. Bolt it.
PERRY. No! Just because I need less than you doesn't mean I don't need something! I need something! Just not that much! Not too much! (*Pause.*) I've had friends, I've had... I even loved someone once. It's the way I am—it doesn't work. It goes so far and then...
LOIS. They leave? (*HE laughs.*)
PERRY. That would be touching. No. I leave. All right? Do you understand?
LOIS. No.
PERRY. I leave.
LOIS. Why?
PERRY. Because I hate this!
LOIS. What?
PERRY. This! This moment! What we're doing. I can't do it. I won't.
LOIS. So we're not friends anymore? Because I saw your cow and you saw my anxiety attack? (*Pause.*) I won't tell if you won't tell. (*Pause.*) Fine. (*SHE starts to exit.*)
PERRY. Is it too late for *Grand Hotel*?
LOIS. Sure, absolutely, let's go to the movies.
PERRY. (*Pause.*) I hate missing the beginning.
LOIS. Why would I want to go to the movies with you?

PERRY. Because by the time it's over we'll feel better. And we'll say goodnight. Instead of avoiding saying hello for the next two weeks.
LOIS. Oh Per.
PERRY. Don't.
LOIS. We get butter. And no salt.

(SHE exits. As HE follows, LIGHTS down on the studio and up on ...)

Scene 5

Selma's apartment, late May. Evidence of money and liberal taste—African sculpture, American Indian rugs, etc. It's raining. PERRY and JAX enter carrying heavy picnic hampers. THEY're both somewhat wet.

JAX. Should we put it away? The perishable stuff?
PERRY. It would have sat out if it hadn't rained.

(PERRY exits to his bedroom. JAX lights a cigarette and stands by the open door, fanning the smoke out into the hall. PERRY enters, having changed into a dry T-shirt and put a Mozart string quartet on his CD player.)

PERRY. You don't have to do that.
JAX. She's in a bad enough mood as it is.
PERRY. Would you like a beer?
JAX. Thank you.

(PERRY gets two beers, gives one to JAX at the door. HE wanders over to the window, gazing out. After a moment.)

JAX. I appreciate you spending so much time with Lois. When she's alone she calls me at the bar and if I don't give her exactly what she needs exactly when she needs it, no matter if it's last call and they're lined up eight deep screaming for my attention, she goes moody on me, hangs up, won't answer when I call back. If she'd just come in with me sometime. But no. She'd blow her cover.

(*PERRY stares at her blankly.*)

JAX. Some gay woman might find out she's gay.
PERRY. But she's not. That is she doesn't identify with the larger picture.
JAX. It'd be easier on her if she did.
PERRY. Would it?
JAX. In the long run.

(*PERRY turns back and looks out the window*)

JAX. I know she doesn't like me working there. Name another job that's gonna understand when I say my girl friend just had a baby and I need the next couple days off. She doesn't think of these things. Would you believe it took me six weeks to talk her into getting insurance? She was ready to go out and get pregnant without insurance. Not a citizen of the real world, our Lois. She thinks I'm fucking around. Doesn't she. Hey, I'm popular, the girls like me. If they didn't, I'd be making jackshit behind that bar. But that doesn't mean I go humping my brains out every time some girl gives me the nod. I don't. I made a commitment. So did she. (*Pause.*) I should introduce you to my friend Alex. Lois knows him. He's dark, brown eyes, a little taller than me, built like a runner, calves for days...
PERRY. Why are you telling me what he looks like?
JAX. He might be your type?

PERRY. I'm not interested in Lois.
JAX. His name is Alex.
PERRY. You can hear me or not, it's up to you.

(*THEY look at each other a long moment. SELMA enters.*)

SELMA. Why did it have to rain. It would have been so lovely if it hadn't rained.
PERRY. We'll still have fun.
SELMA. No, we won't. Nobody'll have a good time.
PERRY/JAX. Yes, we will.
JAX. Where's Lois?
SELMA. Changing. I could smell those cigarettes all the way down the hall.

(*JAX exits. SELMA unpacks the picnic—it's clear that SHE's annoyed with Perry. PERRY tries to help her but nothing he does pleases her. HE puts a finger into the paté to taste it and SELMA slaps his hand.*)

PERRY. Ow!

(*SELMA is silent, unpacking. Pause.*)

PERRY. There's a new 12-step program for people who talk too much. It's called On-and-On-and-On-Anon.
SELMA. What you do with your evenings is your business. You're just renting a room here. We'd discussed the menu. You knew I was planning to cook last night. If the paté isn't seasoned properly, well, it's your life.
PERRY. I was proctoring the sixth grade school play.
SELMA. Until midnight?
PERRY. I redid the bulletin boards outside the library.
SELMA. I just hope to hell you're being careful. (*SHE puts some paté on a cracker and hands it to Perry.*) What do you think?

PERRY. I'm sorry I worry you.
SELMA. About the paté.
PERRY. Excellent.
SELMA. The clinic called right in the middle so I couldn't remember what I'd added and what I hadn't. Alphonso's parents won't take the body. I don't know what's wrong with people. I suggested they have him cremated, I offered to arrange it, to ship the ashes. No. His fingernails were always pink, like they'd been dipped in merthiolate—he just loved pistachio nuts. That baby is life. They don't realize that.
PERRY. Not from that perspective, no.
SELMA. Not from any perspective. Do you know what it costs to raise a child properly? Hundreds of thousands of dollars.
PERRY. (*With her.*) Hundreds of thousands of dollars.
SELMA. You think Lois is going to invest in zero coupon bonds so that child can go to college some day? You think bartending will pay for orthodontia and music lessons and summer camp?
PERRY. I think you should talk to them first.
SELMA. The bonds are in the baby's name. Designated for Lois' child. Of course if anything happens, they'll revert back to me.
PERRY. You went ahead and did it?
SELMA. College tuition has to be paid before the child can register. The baby won't be born until September. If I'd waited until then, they'd mature too late. What.
PERRY. They may feel it's an invasion of privacy.
SELMA. You'd rather that child grew up hanging out in bars? Playing in compost heaps? You who went to Choate?
PERRY. Just be prepared for them not to like it.
SELMA. They won't even know.
PERRY. When you have a piano delivered and send the child away to the mountains for the summer...

SELMA. The piano will be delivered here. And they won't begrudge the child two months in the country. Not when it means they have two months to carry on however they please. And as for the college tuition, it's a done thing. Now we just have to finance a suitable prep school. (*Pause.*) Choate takes girls these days, don't they? (*Pause.*) It's not like you'd be taking the money for yourself. And think how happy it'd make your mother. You've earned it—you survived your childhood. Give it away but take it.

PERRY. More wine?

SELMA. She's not going to public school. I don't care how brilliant your bulletin boards are.

PERRY. She'll go where they want her to go.

SELMA. She'll go where *she* wants to go.

LOIS. (*Off.*) I'm so fat. (*Entering with JAX in tow.*) My skin is screaming.

JAX. If you'd try the vitamin E oil...

LOIS. I'd be fat and greasy. I'm starving.

SELMA. Almost ready.

LOIS. Can we make lemonade? We always had lemonade on Memorial Day.

PERRY. (*Sitting next to Lois.*) So did we.

SELMA. I've got lemons. I may even have grenadine.

JAX. How long does it take to do marshmallows in the microwave?

SELMA. If you promise to be careful you can do them over the hibachi.

JAX. You have a hibachi? Selma, you've been holding out on me.

SELMA. On the fire escape. It's illegal so be careful.

JAX. On eggs I'll walk. What's that?

LOIS. (*To Perry.*) The Juilliard?

(*HE nods.*)

SELMA. Artichoke paté. And wild rice salad, squab...

JAX. What the hell did you do?

SELMA. We were going to New Haven.

JAX. Ah yes. The last bastion of civilization. Although for my money, West Hartford is nicer.

SELMA. Believe me, if I could afford a house in West Hartford...

LOIS. You don't want to move to West Hartford.

JAX. You could always get a job.

SELMA. I have a job.

JAX. A paying job.

LOIS. What Selma does is very important.

JAX. I'm not saying it isn't. She's complaining about money. You need money, you get a job.

LOIS. She's not complaining about money.

SELMA. I live here because I want to.

JAX. You live here because your parents won't visit here.

SELMA. Obviously my parents have no say in where I live.

JAX. That's tough talk from a girl on an allowance.

SELMA. (*Throwing the marshmallow bag at her.*) Marshmallows.

JAX. (*Catching it.*) Per, you wanna do the honors?

(*PERRY gets up and goes to start the charcoal. JAX joins him at the window.*)

JAX. You guys get sticks.

SELMA. If you knew anything about estate management...

LOIS. (*The picnic.*) This looks wonder...

SELMA. (*Overlapping.*) ... you'd know that the best way to avoid probate is to transfer funds before the fact.

LOIS. I'm sorry we didn't get a chance to visit the clinic.

SELMA. Why bother. They all die.

LOIS. Cloth napkins. Lovely.

SELMA. And if there weren't people who could afford to volunteer, they'd have to die alone.
LOIS. This is fun. Really. I'm almost glad it rained.

(During this last, JAX becomes suddenly very still at the window, having seen something across the street.)

PERRY. What?
SELMA. Don't tell me. It stopped raining.
PERRY. No.

(JAX approaches Lois privately.)

LOIS. What is it?
JAX. He's across the street.
LOIS. Who?
JAX. You know goddamned well who. He's watching the apartment.

(PERRY looks out and spots him.)

LOIS. Oh my God.
SELMA. What?
LOIS. Let's just go downstairs.
SELMA. You haven't eaten a thing.
JAX. Downstairs is where he's watching.
SELMA. Either tell me what's going on...
JAX. Or what, Selma. We don't get any squab?
LOIS. That was unnecessary.
JAX. This is all unnecessary. If you'd done what you were supposed to in the first place...
PERRY. He's gone... Sorry, he just came out of Bardino's with a cup of coffee.
SELMA. I'm calling the police.
JAX. No.
SELMA. I'm not sitting here scared to death.

LOIS. There's nothing to be frightened of, Sel. It's the father, he's come around before...
JAX. (*Over.*) Will you shut up.
SELMA. You know him?
JAX. Thank you very much.
LOIS. You expect her to slice paté while you freak out over someone watching the apartment?
JAX. I specifically asked you not to tell her.
SELMA. I thought you had artificial insemination.
LOIS. I couldn't. I can't even choose clothes from a catalogue.
SELMA. So how...
JAX. The stork, Selma, we have a contract with a giant flying bird. Can we go.
SELMA. You slept with some man?
JAX. Oh Christ.
LOIS. It was only once and it really wasn't... I didn't mean... He found out. About the baby.
SELMA. And he's outside my apartment, watching me?
JAX. No spud head, he's watching *us*. Why the fuck would he be watching you.
SELMA. This is awful. (*Heads for the door.*)
JAX. Where're you going?
SELMA. I'm going to go get him.
JAX. No, you're not.
SELMA. We have to talk.
LOIS. Maybe we should.
JAX. This is none of her business.
SELMA. Everyone else seems to know about it.
JAX. No one knows about it.
SELMA. Perry...
PERRY. No.
SELMA. You knew who he was. You recognized him.
PERRY. It's raining. There are not many young men gazing up at this apartment.
SELMA. I want to see him.
JAX. (*Blocking her.*) No.

SELMA. Don't be ridiculous.
LOIS. Sel, come sit by me.
SELMA. (*Sitting reluctantly beside Lois.*) You're just putting it off.
LOIS. It'll be all right.
SELMA. (*To Lois.*) How could you do such a thing.
LOIS. It's ok. Don't worry.
SELMA. It's not, it's...
PERRY. He's gone.
JAX. Light the fire.
PERRY. You still want...
JAX. He's not changing my life. Selma, get Lois some hot tea.
LOIS. Lemonade. Pink lemonade.

(*As SELMA gets up and goes to the kitchen, LIGHTS change to ...*)

Scene 6

Jax and Lois' apartment. It's the fourth of July and FIRECRACKERS can he heard and FIREWORKS seens through the window. The front door opens and PERRY enters and crosses through to the bathroom. HE's swung the front door shut but it hasn't latched because ... Henry's foot is in the door. HENRY enters carrying a bassinet and baby toys. HE exits. PERRY enters from the bathroom with the watering can as HENRY enters with his luggage.

PERRY. What the...

(*HENRY looks up at him for a moment.*)

PERRY. Oh. (*HE watches as HENRY sets up the bassinet—complete with floor length lace cover.*) Are they expecting you? (*HENRY's silent.*) I just thought... It's very warm, isn't it...
HENRY. Do it.
PERRY. I beg your pardon?
HENRY. Water them. Go on.
PERRY. Yes. Of course. (*HE starts watering.*)

(*HENRY takes several stuffed animals out of the bassinet, places them around the apartment. HE tries to hang a little bird mobile. PERRY watches him.*)

PERRY. I have my children make them. Mobiles.
HENRY. When will they be back?
PERRY. Would you like me to give them a message? I'm sure they'll want to thank you for your gift. Do they know where to reach you?
HENRY. Do you know who I am?
PERRY. (*Hesitates.*) We haven't been introduced, have we. I'm Perry, I live...
HENRY. I know where you live.
PERRY. (*Starts to exit.*) This is none of my business. If I can be of any help... you know where I live.
HENRY. You'd think they'd fix it up a little.
PERRY. Perhaps if you left a note...
HENRY. I'M NOT LEAVING! (*Pause.*)
PERRY. Good night.
HENRY. I feel like a jerk, ok?
PERRY. I'm sorry.
HENRY. You wouldn't?
PERRY. Feel abused? I don't know.
HENRY. Well you would. Fucking women.
PERRY. Please.
HENRY. Look what they're doing!
PERRY. They never meant to hurt you.

HENRY. I look just like my father, ok? And now, that I'm older, I'll lift my fork in a certain way, tilt my head, even sound like him. Just like him. As if I *am* him. For a second. What's he going to do? He's going to be lost.

PERRY. Your father?

HENRY. My kid. My son. Like he's adrift in déjà vu, never knowing what he's feeling, who he is.

PERRY. I think if you're patient...

HENRY. It's been seven months! I don't get in there before he comes... They have control, don't you see that. They carry the babies, they own the family, the home, it all comes from them. We have nothing. We have to strut around, get some money, audition to get in, to get a taste of it. Just a taste. But they own it. Everything warm, everything good, they have.

PERRY. I don't know as I'd agree.

HENRY. Even birds—you can't nest by yourself. Try it. Make dinner, something good, spaghetti carbonara, turn on the radio, light candles, sit down... It's just eating without, y'know, someone.

PERRY. I think, if you'd allow a suggestion... I think this can all be worked out, given time, patience, a little willingness on both sides.

HENRY. Maybe Lois and I. We could do it. I think she's... but the other one's a real cunt.

PERRY. I don't like that kind of language.

HENRY. You know what I mean.

PERRY. No, I don't.

HENRY. You're on their side.

PERRY. No. Lois is a friend. Perhaps I am.

HENRY. You think about it, think about what it means, someone out there I recognize, I feel, but I can't see him or touch him or...

PERRY. A lot of kids grow up without fathers.

HENRY. But I'm *here*.

(*Pause. PERRY goes back to watering the plants, HENRY to his stuffed animals. HE's having trouble removing the price tag from one of them. PERRY gets him a pair of scissors.*)

HENRY. Thank you.
PERRY. There's also Lois to consider.
HENRY. Why? She didn't consider me.
PERRY. You have no feeling for her?
HENRY. I didn't say that.
PERRY. Then you do have feeling for her.
HENRY. Do you?
PERRY. (*Laughs.*) I'm not the issue.
HENRY. But you want me to leave.
PERRY. I think it would be best, yes.
HENRY. For who? For you? So you can water her plants? Have ideas? You have keys.
PERRY. Why don't we both leave. I'll tell her the gifts are from you...
HENRY. You'll tell her?
PERRY. Then leave a note.
HENRY. I'm not leaving. But you can leave. The plants are wet.
PERRY. There is, of course, no reason why you should understand my situation. Nor do you need to. Suffice it to say that as Lois' friend, as Jax and Lois' friend, I think it best for me to keep you company.
LOIS. (*Off.*) You need some help?
JAX. (*Off.*) No. Go ahead. I'm all right. Go on.
LOIS. (*Entering and seeing the bassinet and mobile.*) Oh Perry. It's perfect.
HENRY. For the baby.

(*LOIS stares at him.*)

HENRY. Hi.

JAX. (*Enters carrying several bags.*) I thought I told you to sit.

(*LOIS sits.*)

JAX. Hey Perrywinkle. Whoa. Where's the naked bride.
LOIS. Hon...
JAX. Feet up. It's gorgeous, Perry. A virgin's wet dream. (*SHE takes the bags into the bedroom. LOIS puts her feet up.*)
HENRY. It'll be all right. I'll tell her.
PERRY. Jax!
HENRY. You *shut up*!
JAX. (*Entering.*) What. (*Seeing Henry. To Perry.*) Did you let him in?
PERRY. Not intentionally.
JAX. Out.
HENRY. Would you like some tea? Or milk maybe, that would be better.

(*But JAX has picked up the phone and started dialing...*)

HENRY. What are you doing?
JAX. Yes, I'd like to report a...

(*HENRY pushes down the button disconnecting the call.*)

JAX. Perry, could you call from upstairs, please.

(*PERRY starts for the door.*)

HENRY. You don't want to do that.
JAX. Go on.
HENRY. Who're they gonna believe? She's pregnant. I'm the father. Who doesn't belong here? What's wrong with this picture?
JAX. You're not on the lease.

HENRY. Neither are you.

(*The LIGHTS go out. Enter SELMA carrying a cake bedecked with candles and singing.*)

SELMA. Happy fourth of July to you.
Happy fourth of July to you.
Happy fourth of July to everyone and the baby,
Happy fourth of July to you.
Isn't it beautiful! I love candles. And angel food. Your favorite. (*SHE puts the cake down in front of Lois.*)
LOIS. I wish...

(*As SHE takes a breath to blow out the candles, BLACKOUT. End of Act I.*)

ACT II

Scene 1

Lois and Jax' apartment. The next morning. PERRY's asleep in the living room. The bassinet is still there. JAX, dressed in her bartending duds, is smoking and drinking coffee. LOIS, in a bathrobe, is pouring herself some milk and making Wheatena.

LOIS. It's just for a little while. Jax? Until we need the room. He can paint it, maybe. He offered. You think yellow? Pale yellow? Perry could stencil some, I don't know, birds, bunnies...

(JAX heads toward their bedroom.)

LOIS. Selma's in there.
JAX. What?
LOIS. You had to go to work...
JAX. You promised me he'd be outta here in an hour.
LOIS. He had nowhere to go. He gave up his room. So Perry said he'd chaperone and...
JAX. You slept with Selma?
LOIS. No. She stayed the night. You know how she gets if she thinks she's being left out. And I really did prefer having Perry down here for at least the first night and so, well, it all just worked out.
JAX. Did it.
LOIS. You had to work.
JAX. This is insanity. We do this thing, this private thing, to, to, and suddenly everyone, no, this is simply not it, no. No way, you hear me. No way.
LOIS. It won't be like this, I promise.

JAX. You're right, it won't.

LOIS. I mean Perry and Sel, they'll be upstairs, like always, they will.

JAX. Uh huh. And what about Gonads in there?

LOIS. I owe him something.

JAX. He used you, Lois. He got laid, remember? That's what it was about for him. It wasn't a baby and three years together and a family and goddamnit I will not let you Mother Theresa this totally out of proportion.

LOIS. It's not just what you want and what he wants. I'm here, too.

JAX. What's really going on here?

LOIS. It doesn't change anything.

JAX. No? (*SHE looks at her a moment and then starts opening Lois' robe.*)

LOIS. Jax.

(*JAX kisses her.*)

LOIS. (*Pulls back.*) We have a bedroom.

JAX. Nothing's changed but I can only touch you in the bedroom.

LOIS. We might as well get used to it. After the baby comes we're going to have to be more...

JAX. Closeted?

LOIS. Private.

(*HENRY comes out of the other bedroom and crosses to the bathroom. The SOUND of Henry pissing—very loud.*)

JAX. This isn't gonna work.

LOIS. Yes, it will. Look, it's not that big a deal, really. He has to leave when the baby comes, we'll need the room, so it's just a few weeks. It'll be like we have a roommate. He'll pay part of the rent, help out with the cleaning, schlep groceries. And then when the baby comes, he'll come around every so often to play with her—he can babysit. Maybe even pay child support. Or not. It doesn't matter.

JAX. Do you love me?

LOIS. You're twisting this into some kind of test of loyalty which it isn't. This is about Henry, who's the legitimate father, and then the baby who needs a straightened out home.

JAX. And if it fucks up our life, well, gee whiz, that's not a priority.

LOIS. I'm not saying it isn't hard.

JAX. Thank you.

LOIS. But it's not about you and me. It's like... If two people were married, ok, and they loved each other and they were living, where, in Mississippi during the Civil War—or Nazi Germany. And they loved each other but one of them wanted to hide a runaway slave or an escapee from a concentration camp but the other one didn't. It would create problems...

JAX. So I'm a fascist racist for not wanting Mr. Sperm-On-Tap...

LOIS. No...

JAX. I'll hand it to you—it sounds great. You're right up there with the Freedom Fighters.

LOIS. My point was...

JAX. If you want a straightened out home for the baby, I'm the one you have to get clear with, not Henry.

LOIS. But he's what we're not clear about!

JAX. We're totally clear about him—you feel guilty, I don't. It's what to do about it. And your idea... I'm having a logical discussion about total insanity. This is craziness.

LOIS. From your perspective.

JAX. Settle with him, fine. But don't move him into my house. You wanna call it loyalty, you wanna call it love, I don't care. He can't be here. And if you don't understand why, just do it for me.

LOIS. I can't live like that. Every time we disagree about something...

JAX. Do you want to be with me! I mean really with me. Because it doesn't look like it. You won't consider my feelings, you load up on all these people...

LOIS. I cannot spend my life constantly reassuring you. And you're avoiding the issue.

JAX. Who's avoiding the issue? (*SHE looks at her a moment and then heads for the bathroom.*)

LOIS. Jax, if we can't even agree on this, what are we doing here?

JAX. (*Pounding on the bathroom door.*) Hey, raging bull, hurry up in there.

LOIS. Jax...

JAX. (*To Lois.*) I have to pee, do you mind?

HENRY. (*Comes out of bathroom.*) Good morning.

(*JAX ignores him and goes into the bathroom.*)

LOIS. You want some breakfast, Henry?

HENRY. I'll get it.

LOIS. No, you're the guest. What would you like?

HENRY. Anything. Whatever you're making. (*SOUND of shower.*)

LOIS. How did you sleep?

HENRY. It's a wonderful room for a baby. Quiet, lots of sunshine.

LOIS. Yellow would be nice, don't you think? Pale yellow?

HENRY. Lovely.

LOIS. You'll be considerate of her. Because you can't stay if it gets difficult. What I mean is, it's up to Jax. Whether you stay or not.

(*The TIMER RINGS for the egg. PERRY sits up.*)

LOIS. You want toast with your eggs, Per?

PERRY. Thank you.
HENRY. How was the couch?
PERRY. Fine.
HENRY. It's quiet. For sleeping. A quiet apartment.
PERRY. And you're moving in.
HENRY. You have an objection?
PERRY. It's not up to me.
HENRY. Why would it be.
PERRY. What I'm wondering is why it's up to you.
HENRY. Up to me?! Up to me! None of this was up to me. If it were up to me, this wouldn't be a problem.
LOIS. All right.
HENRY. Up to me.
PERRY. You have heard of birth control.
HENRY. She wanted to get pregnant!
PERRY. In other words you *assumed* that as usual the woman would bear the responsibility...
HENRY. I *assumed*...

(JAX enters from the bathroom in a bathrobe and crosses to the bedroom, shutting the door behind her.)

HENRY. ...I wasn't getting shanghaied, yes, I assumed I wasn't getting robbed, used, taken...
LOIS. You take milk in your coffee, Henry?
HENRY. I take tea.
LOIS. Good. I mean, so do I.

(SOUND of dresser drawers being yanked open.)

HENRY. What does Jax take?
SELMA. *(Off.)* People are trying to sleep.
PERRY. Coffee.
SELMA. *(Off.)* Stop it! What are you...
JAX. *(Off.)* Get the fuck out of my bed! Get out! Get out! Get out!...

(*PERRY heads for the front door.*)

LOIS. Perry, come and eat while it's still hot. It's ok.

(*PERRY hesitates. The bedroom door flies open and JAX, now dressed, pushes SELMA, who's clutching the quilt around herself, out into the living room.*)

JAX. All of you —out!

(*PERRY exits.*)

LOIS. Per, you don't have to...

(*JAX pulls the quilt off SELMA who shrieks—SHE's in a T-shirt and underpants—and runs into the bathroom, locking the door.*)

LOIS. That's just great. Very productive

(*JAX looks at her and exits to the bedroom. SOUND of drawers being yanked open.*)

HENRY. Something's burning.
LOIS. (*Grabbing the pot off the stove, SHE burns herself.*) Ow!
HENRY. Put it under cold water. (*HE puts her hand in some water.*)
LOIS. I'm sorry about all this.

(*The bathroom door cautiously opens and SELMA peers out. Just then JAX enters from the bedroom carrying her pack and dressed to leave. SELMA sees her and slams the door. LOIS and HENRY turn around at the sink.*)

LOIS. What are you doing?

HENRY. She burned herself.

(*JAX looks at her a moment, finally exits.*)

LOIS. Jax, no.

(*SHE tries to go after her but HENRY holds her hand under the water.*)

HENRY. You gotta keep it under the...
LOIS. (*Shoving him aside.*) Let go of me! (*SHE runs to the door and exits to the hall where SHE can be heard calling.*) Jax! Jax, wait. Jax!

(*SELMA enters cautiously from the bathroom, towels wrapped around her.*)

HENRY. She's gone.
SELMA. Thank God.

(*SHE crosses back to the bedroom and closes the door. LOIS enters from outside crying softly.*)

HENRY. What you need is some ice. (*HE goes to the freezer and starts rummaging around. HE pulls out several empty ice cube trays.*) You should fill these. (*HE continues rummaging.*)

(*LOIS crosses to the bedroom but seeing the door shut, glances at the bathroom and exits there, shutting and locking the door.*)

HENRY. (*Pulls the Tupperware container holding the hailstone out of the freezer.*) Lo? Is this ice? Lois? (*No answer. HE smells it—it smells bad—empties it out into the sink. As HE returns to the freezer to rummage for ice, LIGHTS change to ...*)

Scene 2

Three weeks later. Jax and Lois' apartment. It's very late, 3 a.m., and very hot. LOIS, unable to sleep, comes quietly out of her bedroom, dressed in a loose cotton nightgown. SHE's almost eight months pregnant and very uncomfortable. SHE stops at Henry's door and listens a moment—HE's asleep. SHE relaxes and crosses to the kitchen where SHE opens the freezer to get her hailstone. It's not there. SHE searches the freezer, then the cupboard where SHE finally finds the empty Tupperware container. SHE starts to cry but stops herself. SHE thinks she hears Jax coming up the stairs and quickly opens the door.

LOIS. Ja-... Oh. Hi. (*SHE becomes momentarily conscious of her appearance and then rejects the notion.*) You're never out this late.
 PERRY (*Off.*) Sorry to disappoint you.
 LOIS. You didn't. Come in.
 PERRY. (*Off.*) It's late.
 LOIS. Please.

(*PERRY enters. HE's wearing a polo shirt and khakis.*)

LOIS. You want some iced tea?
 PERRY. All right.

(*HE sits while SHE gets him the tea.*)

LOIS. What?
 PERRY. You're... pregnant. (*HE laughs.*)
 LOIS. I'm not that much bigger. You just haven't seen me. For three weeks.

PERRY. I'm sorry.
LOIS. I don't know why nobody believes me. He doesn't change anything. I am still me. The baby is still right here. He's just a person. I don't even really see him—he's working double shifts. Triple when you consider what he does around here. He does everything. The shopping. He cleans the house—look at this place—it's clean. He defrosted the refrigerator which was... He cooks—he's a good cook—and freezes things so all I have to do when I get home is heat something up. He does the laundry...
PERRY. She'll call.
LOIS. She can go to hell. (*SHE starts to cry.*)

(*HE hands her his handkerchief.*)

LOIS. You're such a throwback.
PERRY. It's late.
LOIS. I can't sleep. Nothing's comfortable. And then when I'm finally tired it's time to go to work.
PERRY. You're still working?
LOIS. We need the money. I need the money.
PERRY. You can't work once the baby gets here.
LOIS. I'm going to take a few weeks off.
PERRY. And then what?
LOIS. We'll take turns. What?
PERRY. It's just not how I'd do it.
LOIS. It doesn't much matter how you'd do it because you're never going to get the chance. I'm sorry, that was nasty. I'm sorry. (*Pause.*) She's trying to control me. She thinks I'll want to talk to her so badly I'll ask him to leave. Well I won't. She can go out and work in that bar—we're having a baby. Who's going to have to go to school and hear all this. About how her mother, one of her mothers as if that weren't bad enough, has a motorcycle and gives rides to women named Sid. But if I want the father, the actual father of this child to stay here a few weeks, well, let's just walk out. That's the adult thing to do. What am I doing

with someone who barely made it through community college? In sociology. She won't put her napkin in her lap. Have you noticed? It lies there like a dish towel someone forgot to clear. Once when we were out she put her fingers in her water glass. There has to be some sort of sympathy. It's not enough to want someone, love someone. Not if they can know you so well, know everything and just leave. She knows I can't sleep. She's happy about it. It's what she wants. Fine. Fuck her. She is never going to see this baby. Ever. Do you think she's coming back?
    PERRY. Yes.
    LOIS. Oh Per.

(*SHE starts to cry and goes to him, puts her arms around his neck. It's awkward with her belly and so SHE turns so that HE holds her from behind. SHE nestles into him and rests her head on his shoulder. SHE takes his hands and puts them on her belly.*)

    LOIS. Feel that. Isn't that awful.
    PERRY. No.
    LOIS. You know we're the same. I've only ever loved one woman and you've only ever loved one man.
    PERRY. (*HE laughs.*) You mean we're inexperienced?
    LOIS. (*Pause. SHE faces him, strokes his shoulders, arms.*) No.
    PERRY. (*Pause.*) Yes. (*HE detaches himself.*)
    LOIS. Where were you tonight?
    PERRY. Nowhere. Walking.
    LOIS. At three in the morning?
    PERRY. I couldn't sleep. I should go up.
    LOIS. You haven't finished your tea.
    PERRY. Goodnight.
    LOIS. Ok.

(*As SHE gives him a chaste kiss, HENRY opens his
    bedroom door and gazes at them sleepily. HE's dressed
    in his bathrobe. THEY don't notice him.*)

LOIS. See you tomorrow?
PERRY. Yes. (*HE exits.*)

(*LOIS shuts the door. SHE picks up Perry's iced tea glass.
    As SHE cools her brow with it, her throat ...*)

HENRY. It's hot.

(*SHE freezes.*)

HENRY. Thunder days. That's what my dad calls them.
When the clouds fist up and the air lies down all over you.
Everything waiting, holding its breath...

(*Without looking at him, LOIS quickly exits to her
    bedroom. As HENRY looks after her, LIGHTS change
    to ...*)

Scene 3

*The next afternoon. Henry's bookstore. HE's cataloguing
    books. JAX enters. SHE's in a summer dress and
    sandals. SHE watches him a moment.*

JAX. Henry.

(*HE sees her. HE goes back to work.*)

JAX. Please.

(*HE stops working but stays where he is.*)

JAX. I have no power here. Nothing you want. I can only ask you. She doesn't realize what she's doing. She's frightened. I need to be with her.

HENRY. You need. (*HE goes back to work.*)

JAX. Yes. I need. Maybe we shouldn't have, well, obviously not picked you. I'm sorry. But we were happy. We did this because we were happy. You know what that means. Henry. You can see what's happening. You're not cruel. Please.

HENRY. No.

JAX. I don't like you. I can't help it. It's personal. I'm not good at... I don't know how to do things except straight out, in a straight line. I should probably, because of the way I feel, have some kind of curve ball here, some kind of way to get you to do what I want despite how I feel but I don't. (*Pause.*) Henry, you're not a bad-looking guy. You're... clean. You could get a girlfriend. There's no percentage hanging around a pregnant lesbian. And making use of how guilty she feels—it's not noble.

HENRY. She's sick. She could lose the baby.

JAX. (*Pause.*) What do you mean she's sick.

HENRY. She's worn out. She can't eat, she can't rest. She looks awful.

JAX. Has she seen the midwife?

HENRY. No.

JAX. Then how do you know she's sick.

HENRY. I'm there. I didn't walk out.

JAX. Selma's got a good g.p. Ask her to...

HENRY. She doesn't want Selma, she wants... She's not thinking clearly. She forgets things. She doesn't pay attention. She got on the wrong bus the other day. We had to go pick her up. She was helpless, in tears, like a little child...

JAX. Henry, if nothing else convinces you. You've gotta go. You've gotta let me back in. What's the point if she loses the baby. Then you'd have nothing.

HENRY. Look, I didn't ask for this, ok? I mean it should be clear that I wouldn't go out and get two homosexuals to raise my child. Wait. Now, you have your life, Lois has hers, you're living the way you want, you're adults, fine. In this country everyone's entitled to their own thing no matter what it does to them...

JAX. This isn't about lifestyle, this is about Lois, the baby...

HENRY. My baby. Mine. And there's nothing you can say—miscarriage, love, crying—nothing that'll get me outa there. Because my kid, any kid, needs more than just women. You cannot show him only half of life.

JAX. Wait a minute...

HENRY. I have work to do. (*HE goes back to his books.*)

JAX. You mean if Lois was married to a man. And they wanted a kid but he was sterile so she went to McGonnigal's and met you and got pregnant...

HENRY. No man would let his wife go out to a bar and...

JAX. Humor me. You met Lois, you tracked her down. What would you have done?

HENRY. What do you mean—when I got to the apartment and saw, what, a man there?

JAX. And you found out he was sterile.

HENRY. Why would I think that? His wife's pregnant.

JAX. You were the one who wanted to talk principle, Henry. How you found out, who, what, where, it doesn't matter. Based on he's sterile, she's pregnant, it's your kid, then what.

HENRY. Jax, it just doesn't apply.

JAX. Why.

HENRY. She's married.

JAX. So even if it was your kid, if Lois was living with a man, you wouldn't move into their house?

HENRY. (*Pause.*) Maybe she'd like living with a man. Maybe you'd like it.

(*SHE comes close to him, smiles, stares him down.*)

HENRY. Maybe not.

(*SHE laughs, exits. As HE goes back to work, LIGHTS change to ...*)

Scene 4

(*Jax and Lois' apartment, a few hours later. HENRY is vacuuming. There's a BANGING on the door. HE stops the vacuum, listens ... nothing.*)

HENRY. Who is it?
SELMA. (*Off.*) Me!
HENRY. Sorry. (*HE opens the door..*) I couldn't hear you over the...
SELMA. You know I should have a key. Lois could be lying in here, doubled up in labor...
HENRY. She isn't home.
SELMA. I'll copy yours. (*SHE holds out her hand.*)
HENRY. Did you need the vacuum back? I didn't mean to keep it so long but once I got started. Her carpet sweeper just can't manage these floors. You see all those cracks?
SELMA. It doesn't work on me, Henry.
HENRY. What doesn't work on you. (*SHE takes back her hand.*)
SELMA. Keep the vacuum.
HENRY. But it's new. Almost new.
SELMA. Lois needs a vacuum. I'll buy another.
HENRY. You'll just go out and buy...
SELMA. You want to give this one to Goodwill, fine.
HENRY. No. Thank you.
SELMA. It's for Lois.

(*There's A KNOCK at the door. THEY look at each other. THEY whisper.*)

SELMA. Would she knock?
HENRY. Jax, you mean.
SELMA. Why would Lois knock.
HENRY. Why would Jax knock.
SELMA. She hasn't been back, called, anything?
HENRY. No. Not really.
SELMA. What do you mean not really.
HENRY. She hasn't called Lois that I know of.

(*There's another KNOCK at the door. THEY look at each other. HENRY answers it. It's PERRY, carrying an old shopping bag. HE's wearing flip-flops.*)

PERRY. Hello. (*Seeing Selma.*) Oh. Hi.
SELMA. What are you doing here?

(*PERRY laughs, shakes his head.*)

SELMA. What's that? (*The shopping bag.*)
PERRY. I didn't think anyone was here.
HENRY. We thought you were Jax.
SELMA. Why would Jax knock.
HENRY. She wouldn't.
PERRY. She might.
SELMA. You think she's coming back?
PERRY. Yes, of course.
SELMA. Why "of course"?

(*PERRY doesn't answer.*)

HENRY. I think... Of course I don't know... If things stay the same...
SELMA. They won't if she comes back.

HENRY. What I meant, if there's enough time, if things get a chance to normalize... I'm making life a lot easier for her.

SELMA. We're all making life easier for her.

PERRY. Does she want it to be easy?

SELMA. She doesn't know what she wants which is why we have to focus on the child. Whatever is best for the child. And if I may be frank, if I may tell the truth here and trust it will go no further... (*SHE looks from one to the other.*)

HENRY. Tell the truth.

SELMA. I think that child would be much better off if Jax were to decide to stay where she was. There. I've said it.

HENRY. Everybody knows that.

SELMA. Thinking it and saying it are two different things. And doing something about it, well, that's yet another thing.

HENRY. You want to do something about it?

SELMA. Do you?

HENRY. Like what?

(*PERRY laughs.*)

HENRY. What's so funny?

(*PERRY shakes his head.*)

HENRY. He's going to tell her. What's he going to tell her.

SELMA. Perry, do you really think it would be for the best if Jax returned?

PERRY. I have no opinion.

SELMA. Don't be absurd. You have to have an opinion.

PERRY. I don't know whether it would be good or bad if Jax returned.

HENRY. Because you assume that no matter what happens, Lois will still come whispering to you.
PERRY. She doesn't come whispering to me.
SELMA. He's right. If they really got back together, there'd be no more secrets.
PERRY. Good.
HENRY. What's in the bag?
PERRY. Nothing. I was on my way home.
HENRY. In bare feet? (*Grabs the bag.*)
PERRY. It's nothing. I needed some glue.
HENRY. (*Takes out the cow marionette.*) A puppet? He doesn't want puppets.
PERRY. It's for Lois. And it's a marionette. Named... (*HE falls silent.*)
HENRY. You named it?
SELMA. (*Takes the marionette, puts it back in the bag and hands it to Perry.*) Of course it may be that Lois would be unwilling to give up confiding in Perry. She's very fond of him.
HENRY. He kissed her last night.
PERRY. I'm not going to dignify this.
HENRY. Dignify? You kiss a pregnant woman in a nightgown...
SELMA. I'm sure Lois was just saying goodnight.
HENRY. You're sure? You were there?
LOIS. (*Enters.*) Well. Hi.
SELMA. It's the whole family.
PERRY. Almost.
HENRY. Look what Selma gave us. Isn't it wonderful. (*HE turns on the vacuum.*)
LOIS. (*Over the noise.*) I thought we just borrowed... Henry?
HENRY. (*Shutting it off.*) Isn't it great.
LOIS. Are you sure you want to...
SELMA. It doesn't have the attachment I need for the carpets.
LOIS. Let me at least pay for...

ALL No.

LOIS. I am working.

SELMA. If you didn't want it, I was going to give it to Goodwill. While we're all here, when are we going to paint that room?

HENRY. What room?

PERRY. The baby's room.

SELMA. If we can set a time...

HENRY. We have plenty of time...

LOIS. I promised Jax she could paint the room.

SELMA. I'm sure you did but... (*SHE gestures—Where is she? Pause.*)

HENRY. When it's time, I'll paint the...

LOIS. (*Picking up the vacuum and taking it to the door.*) I don't want it. Thank you anyway.

SELMA. It hurts. We've all been through it.

(*LOIS opens the vacuum cleaner, takes out the bag and starts emptying the dust out onto the floor.*)

HENRY. Whoa whoa whoa. (*HE takes the bag away from her, puts it back in the machine and vacuums the dust back up.*) We can always make more dirt.

LOIS. Take it away.

SELMA. This is silly. Henry told me himself what a help it's been. He's doing all the cleaning.

HENRY. Whatever Lois wants.

LOIS. (*To Henry.*) If Jax were Martha Washington and I were Madame Curie, would you have moved into our house?

SELMA. (*Pause.*) Is this a normal question? Lois, sit down.

LOIS. (*Ignoring her.*) I saw her.

SELMA. Who?

LOIS. Just now. At the greenhouse.

PERRY/SELMA. Jax.

LOIS. Maybe she'd like to "live" with a man?

HENRY. Well maybe she would. It's not a crime. Men and women live together. I've seen it.
SELMA. What did she want?
LOIS. (*SHE looks at Henry a moment and then pulls out a wad of cash.*) Rent. All of it.
HENRY. I already paid it.
LOIS. You what?
SELMA. You couldn't come to me for money?
LOIS. You paid the rent?
HENRY. It was getting late, I didn't want to worry you, I didn't want any landlord problems with the baby coming, I am living here. She's not moving back in. Is she? Use her money for baby clothes. Or pay me back. Whatever you want. Is she moving back in?
LOIS. (*Hesitates and then exits to her bedroom, shutting the door. Pause. SHE opens the door.*) And I can get another hailstone. (*SHE slams the door.*)
SELMA. (*Pause.*) It doesn't necessarily mean anything.
HENRY. How the hell do you know what it means! Are you God? Do you know everything?

(*PERRY starts to exit.*)

SELMA. He's yelling at me. Perry, you're just as much a part of this as we are.
PERRY. A part of what.
SELMA. She's Madame Curie and she hates vacuum cleaners and you'd walk out of here? This is a friend? You cannot go through life like a needle. You've got to...
PERRY. Tell me, Selma! Tell me how to live my life! Please!
SELMA. Like that. Just like that.

(*PERRY exits.*)

SELMA. Well, something came out of this.

(HENRY is silent.)

SELMA. As far as you know this is the first time they've spoken in three weeks.

(HENRY nods.)

SELMA. So. It's the end of the month, the rent's due...
HENRY. This has nothing to do with the rent.
SELMA. *(Pause.)* What does it have to do with, Henry?
HENRY. How should I know.
SELMA. All right then. It's the end of the month. Jax is trying to regain her foothold. She doesn't have the courage to come here...
HENRY. I'm going to go to bed.
SELMA. It's not even eight o'clock. Oh, you know what's playing at the Retro? *Now Voyager.* "Oh Jerry, don't let's ask for the moon..."
HENRY. I'm tired.
SELMA. You're probably hungry. I could do a quick pasta...
HENRY. I'm not hungry, I'm tired. But thank you for the vacuum.

(HE exits into his bedroom. SELMA heads for the front door, picks up the vacuum cleaner and exits. A moment later HENRY and LOIS open their doors. Pause.)

HENRY. I thought we'd have shrimp salad tomorrow.
LOIS. Fine. *(SHE exits to the bathroom.)*
HENRY. *(Pause.)* Lois, you've got to protect yourself. I could do that for you.
LOIS. *(Enters and heads for the bedroom.)* Good night.
HENRY. I'm not a crazy person. I didn't track you down because I had some insane notion, some fantasy. You wanted to be with me.
LOIS. Henry, you know why.

HENRY. Why are you denying what happened?
LOIS. Nothing happened!
HENRY. Ok, ok, don't get upset. It's rare, or it's rare for me. The way we were that night. You felt it. I know you did. Of *course* there's a baby, there had to be.
LOIS. What is the point of all this.
HENRY. I haven't seen your eyes since that night.
LOIS. I'm not proud of what I did to you.
HENRY. Do I look unhappy Look at me.

(*SHE does. HE smiles.*)

HENRY. You see?
LOIS. I just think it would be better for everyone concerned if we weren't too familiar with each other.
HENRY. Lois, I've been inside you.
LOIS. Once! One time! And I didn't even come! I'm sorry, Henry, I'm sorry.
HENRY. Why? You were frightened. You wouldn't be next time.
LOIS. There's no next time! There was never going to be a next time! The only reason we could be close at all was because I knew I'd never see you again!
HENRY. But that doesn't make any sense. People spend their whole lives searching for someone to be close to.
LOIS. It's too close! I don't want it! Now goodnight! (*SHE exits into her bedroom.*)
HENRY. (*Looks after her a moment and then crosses to her door.*) Lo? (*HE knocks on the door. There's no response.*) I just want to ask you something. (*There's no response. HE laughs.*) It's probably good there's a door here. Ok. There was this copy of the Joy of, you know, Lesbian Sex in the store. I'm not putting it down, obviously I don't get it. I mean it must be stimulating and so forth but it's not... I mean I'm with a woman, I do all that. All that in the book. And then we, you know, have intercourse. In addition. Of course it's not just sex, I

understand that, but I love you. There're so many reasons why it would be, I mean there's the baby number one... (*SHE locks the door. HE stares at the door.*) Did you just lock the door? Lois? (*HE tries to open the door. It's locked.*) Why did you do that? You think I'm going to... Is that what you think? You came to me, lady. And let me tell you, if I had it to do over again, I would never, I mean never pick you to be my mother, the mother of my child. You came to me. I don't do that. I don't force myself. Not like that. What the hell is your problem. (*SHE opens the door.*) Why did you let me stay here?

LOIS. I didn't want to.

HENRY. Then why.

LOIS. For the baby. (*SHE puts her hand on her belly.*) Because you're her father. I'm sorry. (*SHE starts to cry.*)

HENRY. Hey, hey, no. I'm not. I'm not sorry. This is the closest I ever got. (*HE puts his hand on her belly.*)

LOIS. (*SHE allows it for a moment.*) Good night. (*As SHE exits into her bedroom...*)

HENRY. Lois, is she coming back?

LOIS. Yes. She is. (*SHE exits to her bedroom.*)

(*HE looks after her a moment and exits to his bedroom as LIGHTS change to ...*)

Scene 5

The New Haven Green, two weeks later. THEY've all assembled to have a picnic and hear the New Haven Symphony play the "1812 Overture"—with cannon. PERRY and HENRY are spreading the picnic blanket as SELMA supports LOIS. JAX is still offstage. The concert has started and MUSIC can be heard faintly.

(*Music cue.*)

HENRY. Wait a minute, there's a stone...

SELMA. We really did have a huge breakfast. Brunch really. Didn't we, Perry.

PERRY. I'm hungry.

SELMA. Well I'm not. Heat rises. I would have been happy to have taken whatever it is she prepared in the Saab with us—or you and Perry could have taken it. Although why five people need three vehicles to come to one picnic... And a motorcycle. All that exhaust billowing up. A paper bag is no protection from carbon monoxide poisoning. Or salmonella.

LOIS. She worked very hard on this and if you say one word...

SELMA. Coming to New Haven was my idea. Why would I say anything.

HENRY. I thought it was Jax' idea.

SELMA. I arranged months ago for us to come here on a picnic.

PERRY. It rained.

SELMA. Was that my fault? You were there, Henry, weren't you? I could have sworn you were...

LOIS. Jax chose this spot and this concert to please you, Selma. And you're going to have a good time. All of you. Because if you don't... I need you to do this for me. Please.

SELMA. Why you even let her speak to you. Those women she's living with are lesbians.

LOIS. Meaning?

SELMA. You are so naive.

PERRY. They've started.

SELMA. Lois, sit down, no one can see through you.

(*HENRY moves to help her.*)

LOIS. I'm all right. (*SHE lowers herself and sits back to back against Perry.*)

SELMA. Perry, turn around so that Lois can see.
LOIS. I'm fine. I just want to listen.

(JAX enters laden down with grocery bags. HENRY jumps up to help her.)

JAX. Thank you. *(SHE collapses, her head in Lois' lap.)* Wake me up when they get to the puffa puffa rice part.
SELMA. You're going to sleep?
JAX. Just resting. Move that baby.
LOIS. Sorry, not much lap left.
SELMA. *(Pause.)* People are hungry. Perry's hungry.
PERRY. I'm fine.
SELMA. You just said you were hungry.

(Pause.)

JAX. *(Sitting up.)* Henry, you want to pass me that bag—that one.
HENRY. Can I help you serve anything?
JAX. Nope, it's all under control.

(LOIS throws her a look.)

JAX. You can pass out the napkins.
SELMA. Paper.
JAX. Best thing for a picnic. Ok, we've got your fried chicken, your potato salad, your deviled eggs...
SELMA. Your stars and stripes layer cake...
LOIS. Selma.
SELMA. Can't I make a joke?
PERRY. Wings for me. And an egg or two.
HENRY. The potato salad looks great, you should have some.
JAX. *(Handing the plate to Perry.)* He doesn't want any.
HENRY. It wouldn't hurt him to try it.

JAX. You try it.

(*Pause.*)

LOIS. A breast for me if there's enough and a little of everything else.
PERRY. This is wonderful, Jax.
LOIS. She's a wonderful cook.
JAX. No, I'm not.
LOIS. Yes, you are.
JAX. (*Handing a plate to Lois.*) I can make a couple of simple things. Selma?
SELMA. Nothing for me, thank you.

(*PERRY, HENRY and LOIS, shoot looks at SELMA who refuses to budge.*)

JAX. Henry?
HENRY. Lots of everything.

(*Pause.*)

SELMA. Do you have any cheese?
JAX. No cheese.
SELMA. I brought a little brie if anyone...
PERRY. You had to do it.
SELMA. What. Someone might like some. Lois?
JAX. Put it out, Selma, and anyone who wants some can take it.
SELMA. (*Pulling out the cheese, a china plate and a silver knife.*) It's perfectly ripe if that matters to anyone. Did you bring crackers, Jax?
JAX. Put out anything you brought, Selma.

(*SELMA pulls out a basket and crackers, etc. THEY all watch as SHE cuts herself some cheese and begins to eat with obvious relish. JAX hands HENRY his plate.*)

HENRY. This is wonderful, Jax. Really wonderful.
JAX. You haven't tasted it yet.
HENRY. (*HE eats a bite quickly.*) It's wonderful. I love potato salad.

(*JAX moves downwind and lights a cigarette.*)

LOIS. Aren't you going to eat?
JAX. Later.

(*EVERYONE eats and listens to the MUSIC for a moment. SELMA takes out bug spray and sprays.*)

LOIS. Selma! We're eating!
SELMA. You want to get bitten?
HENRY. You could at least have covered the food.
SELMA. *She's* smoking.
HENRY. *She* went over there.
SELMA. Well the bugs are over here.
HENRY. Of course the bugs are over here. This is a picnic. And she worked very hard on it.
JAX. I fried chicken, Henry. I didn't give birth.
PERRY. Can we listen?
LOIS. Please.

(*THEY listen for a moment.*)

LOIS. (*The baby kicks.*) Oh!
PERRY. All right?
LOIS. Just the baby.
HENRY. Let me feel. (*He crawls over and puts his head on Lois' belly.*)

(*JAX observes this.*)

LOIS. It's stopped now.

HENRY. No, I can hear him. He loves the music.

(*JAX exits.*)

   LOIS. Hon? Henry, get up. Jax!
   HENRY. What I do?
   SELMA. Nothing. She's impossible.
   PERRY. You want me to...
   LOIS. No. She'll be all right.
   SELMA. A person in your condition shouldn't have to put up with moods.
   PERRY. Among other things.
   LOIS. I'm fine.
   SELMA. You're exhausted, and that's dangerous for you and the baby.
   HENRY. She doesn't sleep. She waits up for Jax to get off work and call her.
   SELMA. Staying up all night is Jax' idea?
   LOIS. No, I just can't sleep.
   SELMA. And why do you suppose that is?
   LOIS. Because I'm pregnant and it's August and it's hot.
   SELMA. Lois, the tension in your apartment keeps *me* up.
   PERRY. If you don't want to listen, at least show the musicians some respect.

(*THEY listen to the MUSIC for a moment.*)

   SELMA. (*Offering the brie, sotto voce ...*) Anyone? (*No one answers. Sotto voce ...*) Have you picked out a name yet?
   HENRY. Jax is picking it out.
   SELMA. You can't be serious. (*No one responds.*) But it won't have any meaning.
   LOIS. Because it wasn't her egg, her relationship to the child has no meaning?

SELMA. All right. All right. But look at her name. What if she names the child Ajax. It's absurd.
LOIS. The family who took care of her mother when her father walked out on them was Greek. It makes perfect sense and it's a loving memory.
SELMA. But she's so erratic—she could pick anything and think it was funny.
HENRY. Delilah.
SELMA. Exactly.
PERRY. Here it comes. (*The climax of the MUSIC.*)
SELMA. And then the poor child would have to live with it.
LOIS. Do they have a cannon?

(*JAX enters with a slice of pizza and a strawberry ice cream cone.*)

PERRY. From 1812.
JAX. This is New Haven. They do things right. (*SHE gives the cone to LOIS and sits by her. The CANNON goes off.*)
SELMA. Oh!
PERRY. This is the best part.

(*The CHURCH BELLS begin to chime.*)

LOIS. It's lovely.
PERRY. All the churches around the green...

(*The piece ends. THEY applaud.*)

SELMA. Almost makes you want to go to war.
HENRY. (*To Lois.*) Can I have a lick?
JAX. No, you can't have a lick.
HENRY. Sorry.
JAX. Go get your own.
HENRY. Fine.

SELMA. Henry, I brought some tea for Lois. Pour it for her.

JAX. I don't believe you people. She's eating a fucking ice cream cone. It's cold. She doesn't want....

LOIS. Could you help me up, hon.

JAX. ... hot fucking tea.

LOIS. Jax. Help me up.

JAX. (*Helping HER up.*) Are you all right?

LOIS. I'm fine.

HENRY. You need anything? Want me to...

JAX. No, she doesn't want you to. (*To Lois.*) Did you talk to Kate?

LOIS. Not now. Per, could you bring my bag.

JAX. When?

LOIS. I'll meet you at the car. (*Exiting with JAX.*)

(*PERRY gathers up Lois' things.*)

HENRY. What....

SELMA. It's beyond me.

HENRY. (*To Perry.*) Do you understand it?

SELMA. (*To Perry.*) How can she put up with it?

PERRY. They love each other! And all this pettiness about cheese and napkins and ice cream isn't going to change that. When you... I'll see you at home.

SELMA. Finish what you were saying.

PERRY. They won't spend any time with you if you keep making them miserable. (*HE exits.*)

(*Pause. SELMA packs up.*)

HENRY. All I wanted was one lick.

SELMA. I wanted some cheese.

HENRY. And crackers.

SELMA. You expect me to eat ripe brie with my fingers? I may be petty but I'm not a slob.

HENRY. I think you're exceptionally neat.

SELMA. (*Looks at him for a moment.*) Thank you, Henry.
HENRY. Do you think I'm a terrible person?
SELMA. There's no such thing. Hitler.
HENRY. I try to be helpful, clean up, cook. Is there anything else I could do?
SELMA. Why ask me?
HENRY. You're smart about these things. People.

(*SHE stands and goes to him, puts her arms around him.*)

HENRY. (*HE's confused.*) What...
SELMA. Hug.
HENRY. Oh.

(*THEY hug for a long moment, HENRY waiting for her to break it. SHE does.*)

SELMA. You know, I really think it would be better for everyone if you moved in with me.
HENRY. I'll be fine, thank you. Besides you have Perry.
SELMA. Perry's gay.
HENRY. He is?
SELMA. Couldn't you tell?
HENRY. I'm not very good at that.
SELMA. Apparently.

(*THEY both laugh. SELMA starts gathering things up. HENRY pitches in.*)

HENRY. It must be hard coming home to a gay roommate after working in an AIDS clinic all day.
SELMA. What. Perry's a darling, quiet, so polite, little jokes when I'm depressed, always washes his glass—that's what I hate, men who think glasses aren't really dishes and

leave them in the sink. Here. (*Handing him some brie on a cracker.*) It's perfectly ripe.

HENRY. Thank you.

SELMA. You're welcome. If you want proximity, this is the obvious answer. If you want proximity.

HENRY. What.

SELMA. You move in with me.

HENRY. (*Pause.*) When.

SELMA. Now, if you like.

HENRY. You don't think, well, I guess it doesn't matter, it's your apartment, but, I don't know, shouldn't you talk to Perry first? Give him some notice?

(*THEY start folding the picnic blanket.*)

SELMA. He's very flexible. Besides you two get along. One more toothbrush in the glass won't throw old Per.

(*Pause.*)

HENRY. Where would I sleep?

SELMA. I'd never ask Perry to leave. I'm too fond of him.

HENRY. I see.

SELMA. Don't misunderstand me, Henry, I'm not in love with you but given the opportunity, I'll take it.

HENRY. I don't feel that way.

SELMA. You'd rather pick up lesbians in college bars. Forgive me, I'm retaliating.

HENRY. I had no idea you felt...

SELMA. I don't. You're too young and you'll never amount to anything. But if I'm going to smell you in my house... It's as simple as that.

HENRY. Perry doesn't smell?

SELMA. No one's begging you to live with me, Henry. I'm simply offering proximity. That's all.

HENRY. (*Gathering up the paper picnic bag now filled with trash.*) That's the great thing about paper for a picnic. You can throw it all away. (*HE exits.*)

(*SELMA stares after him a moment. As SHE picks up the remainder of the stuff—a huge load—and trudges after him, LIGHTS down on her and up on the entrance to the green—"another part of the forest"—as JAX enters, LOIS in tow.*)

LOIS. The food was good. (*Pause.*) They just haven't seen you for awhile.
JAX. Lois.
LOIS. All right they were awful.
JAX. I'll live.
LOIS. You know Selma. She gets possessive. You just have to ignore her.
JAX. I know.
LOIS. And Perry likes you very much. And Henry, I think, is finally accepting...
JAX. What do you want from me, Lois?
LOIS. You make great potato salad—I'm kidding. What do I want from you. I want you to be happy.
JAX. I want us to get married.
LOIS. I think I'd look a little silly in white, don't you? No, you're right. With the baby coming, we should see a lawyer, draw up papers—wills. Not that we have anything but to establish, what-do-you-call-it, guardianship...
JAX. I want us to get married.
LOIS. Look, I didn't want to bring up Kate's apartment in front of everybody but I'll ask Henry to leave as soon as...
JAX. You have to choose. I want you. And I wanna say it out loud. That you and I are a family. That if something happens to you, I'm the one they call. It's what I need. And if you can't give it to me, I'm gonna find it someplace else.

I have to. It's not that I don't love you, you know I do. But I have to take care of myself.

HENRY. (*Enters.*) Where's Perry?

JAX. We're talking, we're in the middle...

HENRY. Sorry.

LOIS. He parked by Trinity Church...

HENRY. Lois, could you do me a favor? Could you ride home with Selma? I rode here with her.

JAX. You should buy a motorcycle, Henry. Then you wouldn't have to ride with anyone. See you.

LOIS. Wait. Henry, my friend Kate—Jax knows her. She owns the health food store where I get everything. Anyway she needs a subletter. It's a lovely apartment, we've seen it. Lots of light, hardwood floors, a little sun porch... You need someplace to live.

HENRY. Don't you think it's a little early to be thinking of...

LOIS. No.

HENRY. The baby's not even due till...

LOIS. Next week.

HENRY. (*Pause.*) Actually, Selma and I have been talking. I think that might be the best solution.

LOIS. What?

HENRY. I move in there.

LOIS. But what about Perry?

HENRY. He'll definitely have to move out.

LOIS. But where...

HENRY. The health food place.

LOIS. It's so far away.

HENRY. Well, then I certainly wouldn't want it.

JAX. How soon can you move out?

HENRY. I'll talk to Selma. Let me talk to her. (*HE exits to head off Selma. By now the SUN has set.*)

LOIS. Thank you. Thank you very much.

JAX. What?

LOIS. Do you think that's fair? The two of them off someplace plotting...

JAX. And that's my fault?

LOIS. You encouraged him.

JAX. I asked him when he could move.

LOIS. You implied that it was okay to kick Perry out.

JAX. This has nothing to do with Perry. I mean Jesus Christ, I just proposed to you. Doesn't that mean something? Where're you going?

LOIS. To warn him.

(*As LOIS exits, the LIGHTS go down and come up on PERRY as HE enters another part of the park. HE's looking up at the offstage belltower of one of the churches on the Green. It's almost DARK. A shaft of LIGHT from a church window falls on him. ORGAN MUSIC—a Bach fugue—can be heard faintly. LOIS enters and sees him in the shadows.*)

LOIS. Perry?

PERRY. Shh. They're doing vespers...

LOIS. They're throwing you out. Henry's talking to her right now...

PERRY. You're all flushed...

LOIS. Perry, you're losing your home! It's my fault. We'd found this sublet for him but he said he'd go to Selma and Jax is so sensitive I couldn't press it and he's talking to her right now. You have to stop him.

PERRY. Huh. (*HE laughs.*) That hadn't occurred to me. Of course. (*Brief pause.*) They've taken down the bells. You see—the tower's shuttered. They must use a recording.

LOIS. He's taking your room.

PERRY. Then he must need it more than I do.

LOIS. Don't you want to be with me? Near me? When the baby comes?

PERRY. I'll come visit.

LOIS. No! You won't You'll disappear! This is what you've been waiting for—the perfect excuse to back out of

everything. Well, you can't! You're part of my life and I won't let you!
PERRY. Come on. (*HE starts to exit*.)
LOIS. Perry, please, if you're angry with me, if you leave, I can't bear it. Not now.
PERRY. Are you going to be quiet?
LOIS. She wants us to get married.
PERRY. So that's what this is all about.
LOIS. What.
PERRY. She asked you to marry her and you come running after me?
LOIS. You're the only one.
PERRY. Who what. Who what?
LOIS. Who doesn't want me, ok, who doesn't want anything.
PERRY. (*Pause*.) I want what we have. (*HE takes her hand*.)
LOIS. What do I do?
PERRY. Go home.
LOIS. But if you're frightened, then you, it's supposed to mean stop, isn't it?
PERRY. I think if you're frightened it means you're frightened. And then you do whatever you do.
LOIS. I've never let anyone. In. I don't know how.
PERRY. Neither do I.

(*THEY're silent a moment, safe*.)

LOIS. Can I tell you a secret?
PERRY. Mmm hmm.
LOIS. My mother was perfect. (*SHE laughs*.) And it wasn't a secret. (*THEY both laugh for a moment. SHE suddenly gasps with a contraction*.)
PERRY. All right?
LOIS. I don't know.
PERRY. Just relax a minute.
LOIS. Per?

PERRY. Yes?
LOIS. I think she wants to be born.
PERRY. Breathe.
LOIS. Do you hate me for being such a coward?
PERRY. I love you, Lo, I always will.
LOIS. I want to be a good mother. As good as my mother.
PERRY. What do you think. Can you make it back to the car?
LOIS. Promise me something. Swear.
PERRY. What.
LOIS. I don't want them there. They'll fight over the masks, the gowns, the side of the gurney...
PERRY. Breathe.
LOIS. Promise me. *Promise me*!
PERRY. I promise. Now take a breath. We're parked on the corner. We'll call the midwives, have them meet us at the hospital...

(*As HE helps HER off, LIGHTS change to ...*)

Scene 6

A bench in the hospital waiting area, many hours later. SELMA is getting a cheese and crackers snack from the vending machine. JAX is smoking. There's an upstage door leading to the delivery room.

SELMA. Have you ever noticed how on airplanes you'll eat things you normally wouldn't step in?
JAX. No.
SELMA. Have you ever been on an airplane?
JAX. Yes, I've been on an airplane.
SELMA. There are people who haven't been on airplanes.

HENRY. (*In jacket and tie, rushes in with a monstrously huge bunch of flowers.*) She's not done yet?
JAX. Why not a blue ribbon, Henry. A tasteful little medallion she can pin to her nursing bra.
HENRY. She likes flowers.
SELMA. Somebody's going to end up crying.

(*JAX moves away.*)

SELMA. Lets all try, shall we?
JAX. I hate this! She could be. I'm not good at doing nothing. Waiting. Sitting here doing nothing, nothing, while she's... (*SHE spots the vending machine. SHE tries to pick it up. It's extremely heavy.*)

(*THEY watch her.*)

HENRY. Let me give you a hand with that.
SELMA. Henry, come sit by me.
HENRY. I could get some coffee. There's a coffee shop. I'll get some. (*HE puts the flowers down, looks at Jax, picks them up and exits.*)
JAX. You could live with that?
SELMA. He got Lois pregnant.
JAX. Tell me you're on drugs.
SELMA. It's not easy being heterosexual.

(*JAX stares at her.*)

SELMA. I'm joking. He has to have someplace to live. A person has to have someplace to live, am I right? Or else you have people sleeping in the streets.
JAX. Where's Perry gonna go?
SELMA. Nowhere.
JAX. And Mr. Moss?
SELMA. How could I refuse him. He begged me.
JAX. You're gonna sleep...

SELMA. Please. Our Henry will just have to be happy on the couch.

(*THEY wait.*)

JAX. They know we're here. If she needs a transfusion or something. If she needs us.
SELMA. They know we're here. (*SELMA puts an arm around her.*)
JAX. You're not my type.
SELMA. Oh shut up.

(*HENRY enters carrying, with great difficulty, the flowers and a cardboard tray with three cups of coffee and three pieces of pie. JAX takes the tray.*)

HENRY. It got a little wet. Thank you. The pie.
SELMA. (*Taking the tray.*) Just the way I like it.
JAX. (*Picking up one of the dripping cups.*) What do I owe you?
HENRY. It's on the house. Nothing.
SELMA. That's very nice of you, Henry.

(*JAX starts to sip her coffee. HENRY is standing, holding the flowers, staring at the delivery room door. SELMA looks pointedly at Jax.*)

SELMA. Isn't it.
JAX. Have a seat, Henry.
HENRY. Thank you.

(*HE sits, balances the flowers and takes the proffered cup of coffee from SELMA.*)

SELMA. Here you go.
HENRY. Thank you.

SELMA. (*Trying to feed Henry some of the pie.*) It's not as good as mine but...
HENRY. I really don't care for... (*SHE gets it in his mouth.*)
SELMA. Mmmm.
HENRY. It takes a long time. Really, I don't want any more. To have a baby.
SELMA. Just one more bite. If there were anything wrong, they'd have sent Perry out.
HENRY. (*HE looks at her a moment and then violently throws the flowers down.*) He's in there?!
SELMA. What was the man supposed to do. She went into labor. He brought her in and called us as soon as...
HENRY. They have doctors. Midwives. He could have left her at the door. He didn't have to go into the delivery room while they're, she's... Why aren't you in there?
JAX. I don't know, ok? She didn't ask for me. She doesn't need me. She doesn't want me, ok? Are you satisfied? I don't know, I don't know, I don't...
HENRY. I didn't mean...
JAX. Sorry.
HENRY. Look, she wouldn't have turned me down... I mean we wouldn't all be here, it wouldn't be such a mess, if she didn't want you.
JAX. Thank you, Henry.

(*Pause. JAX and HENRY look at each other, both slightly stunned at his admission.*)

SELMA. We're all anxious.
HENRY. This isn't about you, Selma.
SELMA. Because I don't sleep with her, didn't impregnate her, can't sue anybody...
JAX. Nobody's suing anybody.
HENRY. I don't force myself and I don't sue...
SELMA. I love her.
HENRY. and if you don't know that by now...

SELMA. (*Overlapping.*) And let me tell you, when a person loves somebody, that's a contract.
JAX. I don't know, Henry, you sue me, I sue you, we sell it to the networks—the movies! Big money in the movies.
SELMA. That is the most disgusting...
HENRY. (*Overlapping.*) Nobody is making money off of my son.
JAX. Or my daughter.
SELMA. Agreed.

(*THEY all look at each other, finally laughing at the thought of agreement. The door opens and PERRY enters in hospital greens. THEY look at him, holding their breath as HE crosses to Jax, takes her hands.*)

HENRY. What. What happened.
JAX. She's all right?
PERRY. Perfect.
SELMA. (*A prayer.*) Thank you.
PERRY. She was frightened, it all happened so fast—but you got my message...
JAX. Thank you for taking care of her.
PERRY. (*HE hugs her.*) It was miraculous.
HENRY. My son?
PERRY. Is a daughter.

(*JAX bursts out laughing.*)

HENRY. A girl?
SELMA. Oh for heaven's sake, Henry. She doesn't need a penis to play catch.
JAX. Lo's all right, she's really all right?
PERRY. She's ok. She wants to see you.
SELMA/JAX/HENRY. Who?
PERRY. Jax. And then you two.
HENRY. She wants to see me? Us.

SELMA. Of course she wants to see us.

(*A newborn baby is heard CRYING, offstage. THEY pause and listen to it, suddenly laughing.*)

SELMA/JAX/HENRY. We have a baby!

(*As HENRY, SELMA and JAX EXIT...*)

SELMA. What are we going to name her?
JAX. Oh, I don't know. How about Community Property. CP for short.
HENRY. He's not having a weird name. She's not.

(*PERRY's left alone in the waiting room. HE notices the forgotten bouquet. HE gathers it up, smiling to himself, as HENRY enters and takes the flowers.*)

HENRY. Thanks. Are you coming?
PERRY. Congratulations.

(*HE extends his hand to HENRY who takes it after a moment. The LIGHTS begin to redefine the space, leaving them islanded together in tightly focused specials.*)

HENRY. Thank you. And for helping.
PERRY. Lois has asked me to be the godfather, Henry. I'm going to accept. I hope you understand.
HENRY. (*Pause.*) I was thinking about some kind of garden. On the roof. Something where Lois could go and sit with the baby.
PERRY. It's an idea.
HENRY. We could put those lattices they have for roses.
PERRY. A trellis.

HENRY. But over. Like a canopy. So Lois and the baby could have some shade.

(*As the LIGHTS begin to fade...*)

PERRY. And Jax.
HENRY. And Jax. And Selma.
PERRY. (*Simultaneously.*) And Selma.

(*As THEY laugh, LIGHTS down on them—they hold in tableau—and up on LOIS in a hospital gown sitting in a wheelchair as JAX pushes her on. They, too, should be in a tightly focused island of LIGHT.*)

JAX. Selma's looking at the baby.
LOIS. Have you seen her?
JAX. No.
LOIS. She's tiny. Not even seven pounds. But perfect. Ten fingers, ten toes.
JAX. Are you ok?
LOIS. Yes. Are you?
JAX. I've been better.
LOIS. Forgive me? (*SHE holds out her arms.*)
JAX. It's not exactly private.
LOIS. No, it's not.

(*JAX goes into her arms.*)

LOIS. I'm so sorry.
JAX. I shouldn't have pushed. I knew you were scared and what with the baby so soon. But peach, it's never gonna be perfect. Not with me at least. I'm impatient, I lose my temper...
LOIS. Will you marry me?
JAX. Are you serious?
LOIS. I just had a baby. We have to get married.

(*THEY embrace. LIGHTS down on Jax and Lois as THEY hold in tableau and up on SELMA, again in a special, who's holding the baby.*)

SELMA. Hello. Hello, little girl. We've been waiting for you. Yes, we have. And now you're home. And not to worry, I'm going to take care of you. Keep you safe. Forever and ever and ever... (*Sound of the baby SNEEZING. SELMA laughs.*) That's a sneeze! What a good girl. (*SHE wipes the baby's nose with a Kleenex.*) Blow.

(*As the LIGHTS fade on her, they come up on LOIS and JAX as SELMA, PERRY and HENRY join them and embrace the baby. And fade to BLACK.*)

End of Play

Author's Notes

My experience in production with this play at Whole Theatre and then at Circle in the Square Downtown taught me a few things which may save you some trouble and me some heartache.

First, the set. I'm interested in the imaginative shorthand a designer can invent to anchor a scene. Thus I wrote a play which, while it was about "real" people in "real" places, I hoped didn't require the practical and financial obligations of "realistic" scenery.

This proved to be the case. Our director, Susan Einhorn, our designer, Ursula Belden, and I found the following to be true (and designers, please forgive my inaccurate language):

1. Less is more. This may not seem apparent given the "naturalness" of the dialogue and the requirements for working doors and lights and kitchen paraphernalia, but it confirms my particular writing style which focuses on characterization. Character is all the landscape I need. Attempts at "realistic" scenery proved to be burdensome and distracting—competing with the text.

The property plots and ground plans included in this acting edition of the text provide Ursula Belden's solutions to the practical issues and prove to me that practical requirements aren't a stylistic limitation here. On the contrary, Ursula's unit, modular set was delightful, ingenious and theatrical.

2. The action shouldn't stop. As I wrote the play, I envisioned the scenes flowing from one into another. Susan Einhorn achieved this flow by involving the actors as the stage hands made the necessary minimal adjustments between scenes—again keeping the focus on character and sustaining the flow of action.

Second, casting. Given my experience working with agents and casting people on this play, I offer the following cautionary notes:

1. While our productions in New Jersey and New York City were performed by a "white" cast, I feel that every part in this play can be cast without regard to race. (You can tell them the playwright said so.) What's important is simply that the actor, no matter his or her genetic, ethnic, or social background, have the craft and talent to portray the character: Perry is from old money, Selma from new; Henry has had more education than Jax, and so forth.

2. Stereotypes. Jax and Lois are attractive, womanly women. Perry is similarly "neutral" in his personal style. Which is not to say that in life there is anything inherently "wrong" with proclaiming your preference through your style, simply that these characters would be diminished by such shorthand.

3. Because of the character's age (and the first page of the play) we were deluged with Romeos for the part of Henry. Saying, "He's funny!" brought us a wave of stand-up comedians. Try, "We need a young, nice-looking character actor with a terrific sense of humor." That brought us the wonderful Stephen Hamilton, and might work for you.

I hope this his helpful. Godspeed and above all, enjoy.

Costume Plot

LOIS

I.1

Underpants; Add: black/purple print blouse

I.2

Blue slicker, Black rain hat, Turquoise overalls, Belt, White 3 button T-shirt, White socks, Blue and white cardigan, All-in-one (worn thru-out show w/pregnancy pad inserts), Corduroy pocketbook, Black rain boots.

I.3

Strike: Sweater, loosen belt.; Add: Pregnancy pad #1, Tennis shoes.

I.4

Add pregnancy pad #2, Violet floral dress, White cardigan, Kenya bag, White anklets, Tennis shoes.

I.5

Add Pregnancy pad #3, Pink top, Denim jumper, Socks/sneakers-same.

I.6

Add Pregnancy pad #4, white short-sleeve T-shirt, White flowered jumpsuit, socks/sneakers-same.

II.1

White floor-length nightgown, Flowered, sashed robe, Peds.

II.2

Strike: Robe

II.4

Bright blue-green T-shirt, Coveralls, White tennis shoes, White socks, Add Pregnancy pad #5.

II.5

White rayon top, Floral dress, Beige flats.

II.6

Strike: Pregnancy pads; Add: White robe, peds.

JAX

I.1
Blue bath towel; Change to: Grey trousers, White tank top, Red/orange Open front top, Lace up boots (Beige), Grey socks.

I.3
Red/orange top; Add: Pink top w/snap-up front.

I.5
Off-white trousers, Black print top; Sandals, Jean jacket.

I.6
Faded blue jeans, Belt, Turquoise crop top, Sandals, Sunglasses

II.1
Black trousers, White silk long-sleeve blouse, Black socks, no shoes, Black belt; Change to: White terry robe; Change to: White tank top, jeans, Jean jacket, Purple socks.

II.3
Two-piece blue dress, Print sash, Sandals

II.5
Pink rayon top, Harachis, Neck scarf

II.6
Strike: Scarf

SELMA

I.2
Gold raincoat, 2-piece houndstooth suit, Ivory blouse w/tie, Black pumps, Nude stockings (worn thru-out show), Black handbag, Gold jewelry.

I.5
2-piece orange pant suit, White silk tank top, Gold jewelry, White flats.

I.6
Blue and white print sleeveless dress, Red jewelry, White flats, Red & white polka-dot scarf

II.1
Oversize black T-shirt, hair in curlers

<u>II.4</u>
Violet silk skirt, Floral blouse, Beige shoes, slip, Gold jewelry, Belt.
<u>II.5.</u>
White silk trousers, Gold silk jacket, Gold silk T-shirt, White flats, Straw kenya bag, Mexican necklace, Gold earrings
<u>II.6</u>
Strike jewelry.
<u>HENRY</u>
<u>I.1</u>
Bikini underwear.
<u>I.2</u>
Khaki pants, Blue & white striped shirt, Blue tie, Grey sweater vest, Beige desert boots, Belt, White socks (worn thru-out show), Green raincoat.
<u>I.3</u>
Jeans, Striped long-sleeve shirt, Khaki jacket, Black Converse sneakers, Belt.
<u>I.4</u>
Jeans, Plaid shirt, Black Converse sneakers, Belt.
<u>II.1</u>
Blue terry robe, White socks.
<u>II.3</u>
Khaki trousers, White striped shirt, Striped tie, Desert boots.
<u>II.4</u>
Strike: tie.
<u>II.5</u>
Strike: Shirt; Add: Blue 3 button shirt
<u>II.6</u>
Blue shirt, Add: White shirt, Blue print tie, Sports jacket

PERRY

I.2
Green pleated corduroys, Blue shirt, Tie, Fisherman knit sweater, Overcoat—carried, Suede shoes, Black socks, belt.

I.4
Grey plaid trousers, White muscle T-shirt, Blue pullover, White socks, Black shoes, Belt.

I.5
Olive green striped shirt, Buff trousers, White socks, White tennis shoes, Belt.

I.5
Change to: Brown pullover.

I.6
"Old" trousers, Bright blue T-shirt, White tennis shoes, White socks.

II.1
White muscle T-shirt, Grey sweat pants, Tennis shoes.

II.4
White shorts, Bright pink T-shirt, White slouch socks, Tennis shoes.

II.4
Blue jeans, Blue T-shirt, barefoot

II.5
Green & white striped shirt, White jeans, Beaded belt, White socks, Tennis shoes.

II.6
Add: Hospital green surgery coat, Hospital issue face mask.

Property Plot

PRESET:

Light Switches-Down
<u>Selma Unit US Cabinet</u>
Mister w/water
Watering can
<u>Selma Unit DS Cabinet</u>
4 Bamboo trays
<u>US Ottoman</u>
Jax' boots & socks on UL side
<u>DS Ottoman</u>
"Selma" marionette w/head facing SR
<u>Perry Unit</u>
Plants
Ashtray w/water
In SR cabinet: Box of tea bags & 2 mugs on top shelf
Hotpot on bottom shelf w/tea
Cigarettes and lighter in side cabinet
In cabinets: assorted art supplies
<u>Kitchen</u>
Fridge covered
Stove & sink exposed w/Rubbermaid tub in DR corner
Ashtray on stove w/water
Plants
Telephone on counter
In fridge: Milk, Pitcher of Iced Tea, 1 capped Rolling Rock, 2 capped Amstels-on door rack
Under sink: Towel on rack
In cabinet: Top shelf C - 6 tall glasses; Top shelf L - OJ glass; Bottom shelf L - Plates/bowl; Bottom shelf R - Ritz crackers
In top drawer: Selma's ashtray w/water; 2 plastic containers w/lids
In second drawer: Scissors, Cigarettes & lighter

UL Offstage:
Hailstone
Grocery bag - In: paper towels, coffee, carton of orange juice
Car keys
Pink roses
Lois' pocketbook In: biscuits, money
Selma's pocketbook
1 picnic hamper In: 2 wrapped wine glasses, 3 wrapped plastic plates, 1 wrapped china plate, tongs, forks, knives, (wrapped in dinner napkin), serving spoon, paté knife, 4 dinner napkins, decanter of white wine, baguette
1 picnic hamper In: wrapped basket of crackers & breadsticks, wrapped bowl of wild rice salad, wrapped plate of paté, wrapped platter of 4 squab
Grocery bag in: charcoal, marshmallows, kitchen matches, can of lighter fluid

UL Offstage
2 Apartment keys
Bassinet w/lace cover in: 6 stuffed animals, toy truck, GI Joe, Baby mobile
2 laundry bags (Henry's clothes)
4th of July Cake w/candles (matches to light)
2 Beach bags w/towels
Yellow plastic bag for Selma's head
Bath towel
Large wooden tray
Bucket of water & squeeze bottle of water

II
Perry's handkerchief
Bookcart w/books, dust cloth, sandwich board, clipboard, order form, pencil
Wheelchair
"Baby" & Kleenex
"Selma" in shopping bag
Upright vacuum cleaner

Selma's toy (rolling dog)
<u>UR Offstage</u>
Full sheet
3 throw pillows wrapped in Killim
"Herbie" African statue
Bottle of seltzer
Tray holding cup of egg dye, bowl w/pre-blown egg & cake tester, box of food coloring, decals, egg carton w/plastic eggs, 1 empty glass, 1 glass of tea, paper towels
Vending Machine w/cracker snack
Cigarettes & lighter
<u>II</u>
Jax' overnight bag
Quilt
<u>VOM</u> (All Act II)
Perry's sculpture (Act I)
Large bouquet of flowers wrapped in cellophane
To-Go tray holding 3 capped cups of coffee, 3 plastic forks, 5 paper napkins, 3 paper plates holding apple pie wrapped in plastic (top piece eaten)
1 grocery bag In: 10 paper napkins, 5 plastic forks, 5 paper plates, 5 paper cups, pink lemonade in container
1 grocery bag In: container of potato salad, container of fried chicken, container of deviled eggs, plastic serving spoon, plastic slotted serving spoon
Camp stool
Picnic blanket
Selma's bag In: Bug spray, plate of cheese covered w/cloth napkin, basket of crackers covered w/ cloth napkin, silver knife, green thermos
Slice of pizza
Ice cream cone
Box of cigarettes & lighter in grocery bag holding food

Onstage

On side of Left L: Lucite tray holding small lamp (practical), 2 paper wrapped cups, Bar of soap, Ashtray & matches

On "bed": Bottom sheet, 2 bed pillows, Bedspread - folded back from pillows

On floor L of bed: White motel towel

On floor R of bed: Lois' blouse

DR on floor: Bath towel spread out, 2 hand weights

Intermission change over

Strike:

Water can from Perry's unit

Return scissors to 2nd drawer

4th of July cake from Right L

Towel & weights from Perry unit cabinet

Henry's 2 bags

Marionette from DS ottoman (Add bell & put in bag for Act II)

Apartment keys from Selma's Unit

Garbage bag from under sink

Paper towels from under sink

Reposition:

US & DS Ottomans

Stuffed animals—place 2 on US of Right L, the rest on US of Left L

Set:

Smaller hailstone in container in freezer

2 saucepans w/water on stove (1 has lid, the other a wooden spoon)

Measuring cup, box of Wheatena above range on top

1 coffee cup near stove

a 1/2 half full coffee cup on counter above fridge

Package of cigarettes on counter

Lighter w/cigarettes

Jax' shoes to left of DS ottoman

Carton of cigarettes in Perry unit cabinet

2 bed pillows in striped cases on DS of Right L

Put 1" of water in sink Rubbermaid tub
<u>Perishable Properties</u>
Cigarettes
Lighters (Disposable kind)
Ritz crackers
Iced tea
Ginger Ale (for Henry's beer)
Blown out eggs
Hard boiled eggs
Tea Bags
Biscuits
Apple juice (for Selma's wine)
Wild Rice mixed w/brown rice
Melba toast crackers
Breadsticks
Split Pea Soup (for paté)
Cake candles
Baby cereal (in Wheatena Box)
Milk
Orange juice
Pink lemonade
Whipped cream (for Selma's brie)
Potato Salad
Fried chicken
Pink sorbet in ice cream cone (to resemble ice cream)
Cracker/Peanut Butter snack package
Apple pie
Coffee
Carr's Water Biscuits

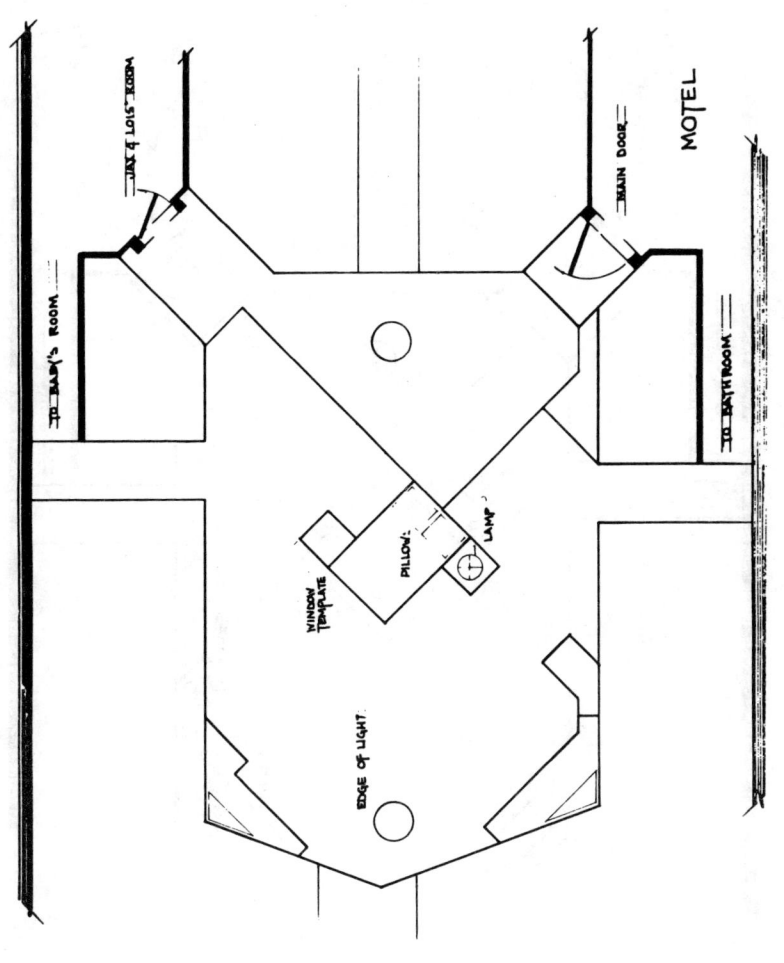

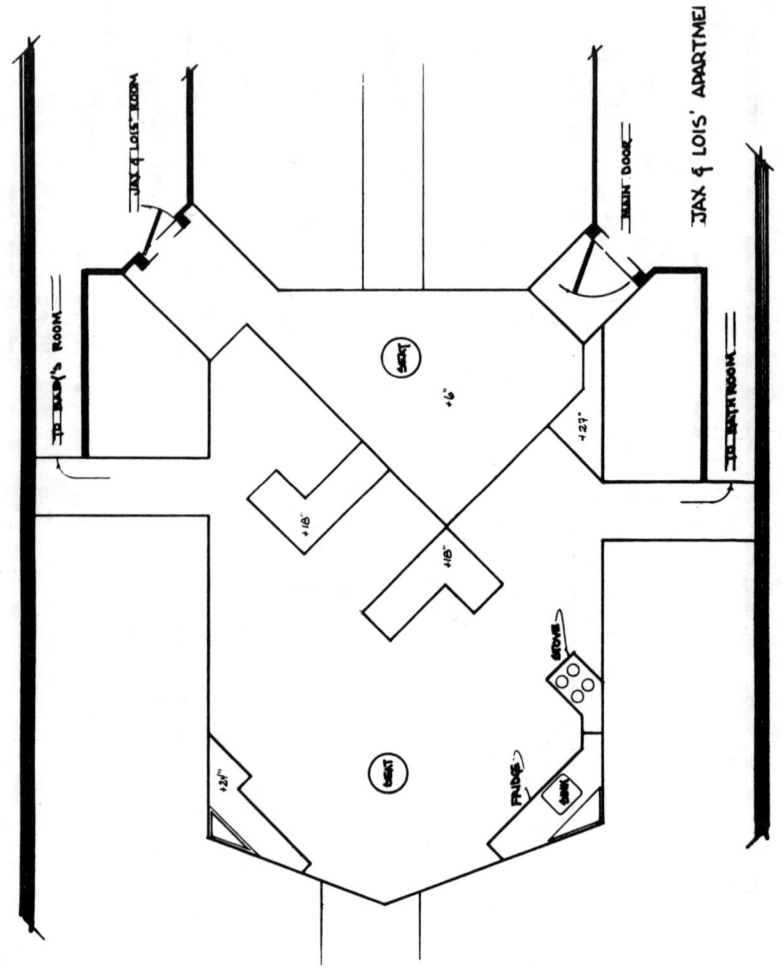

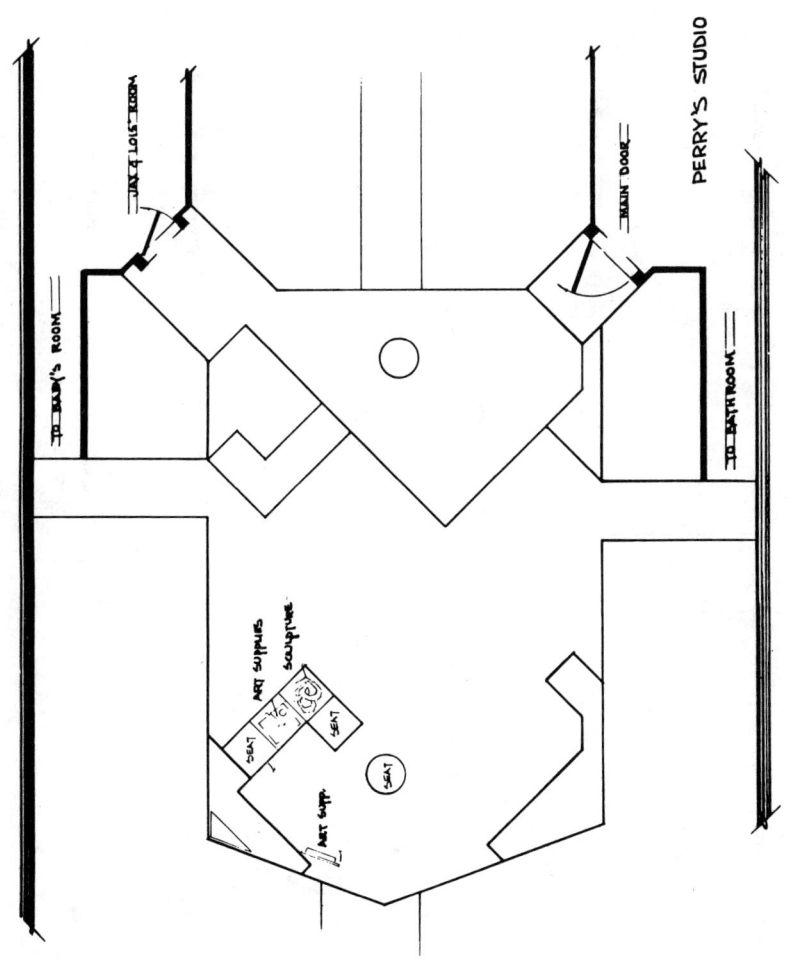

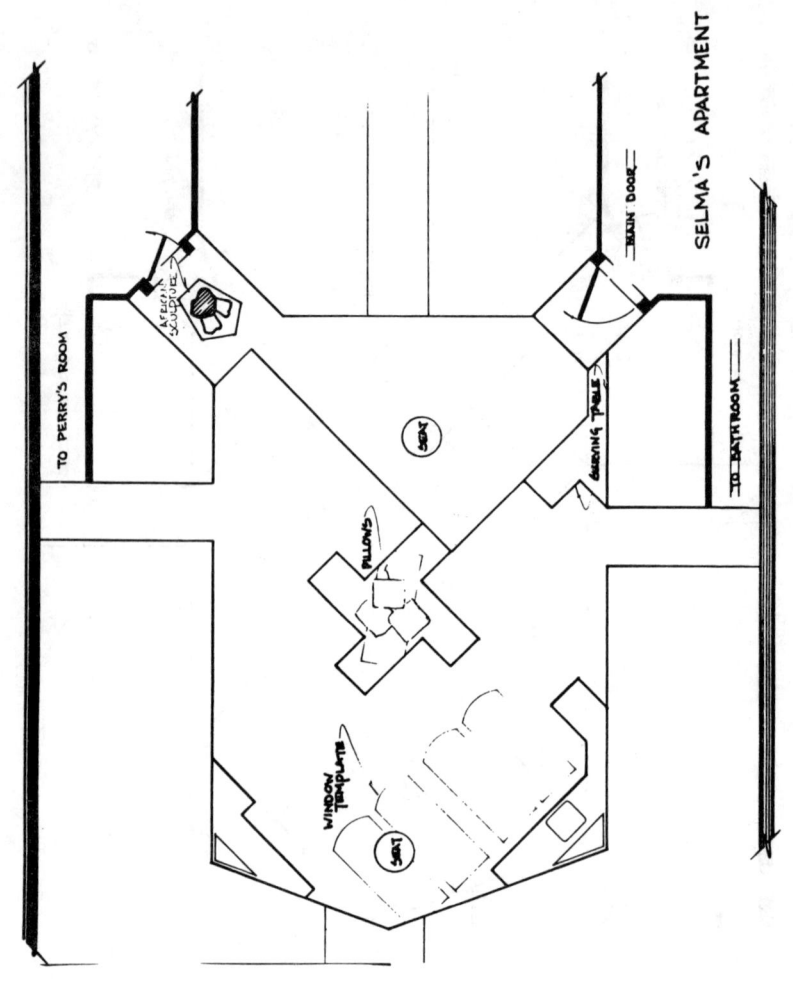

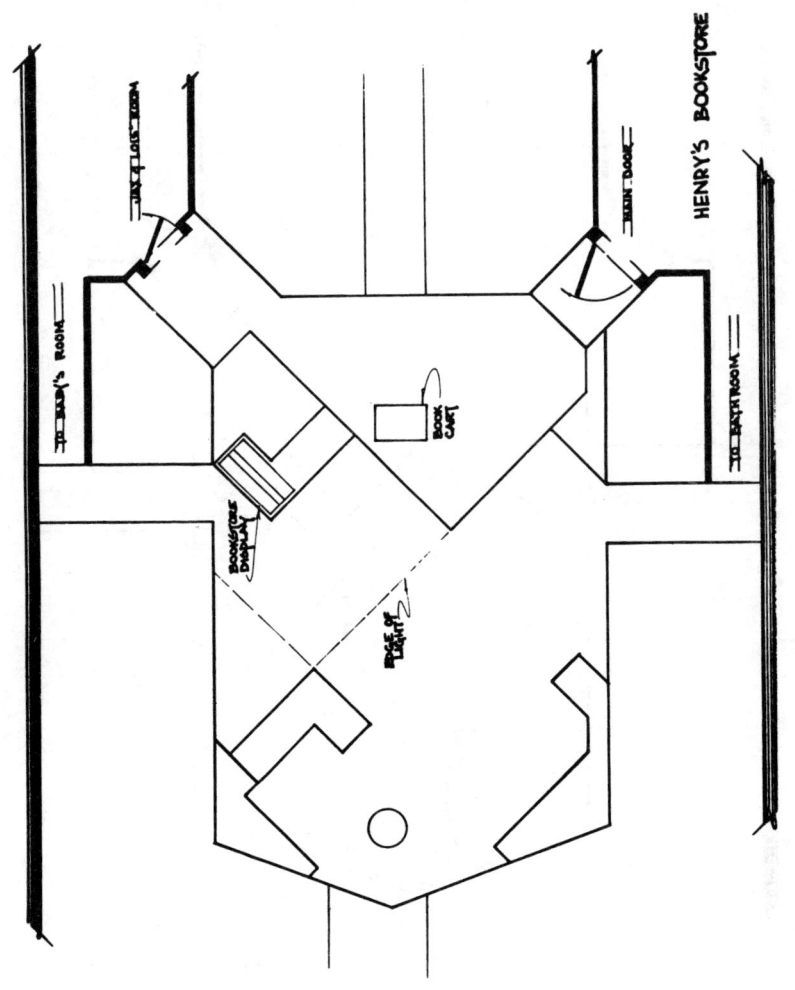

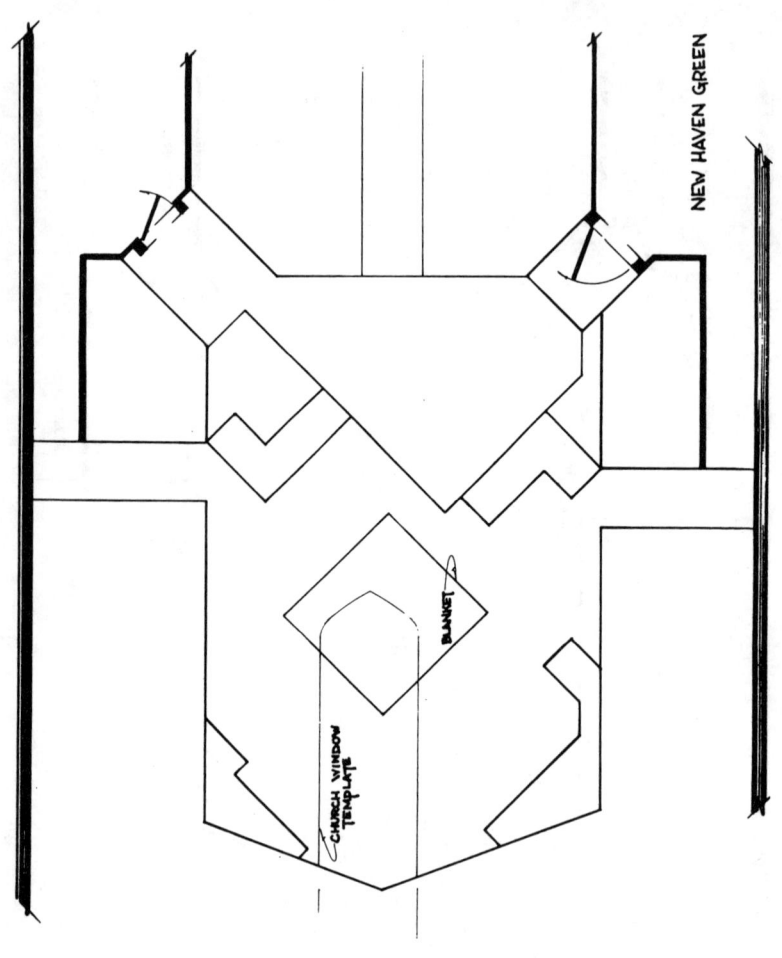

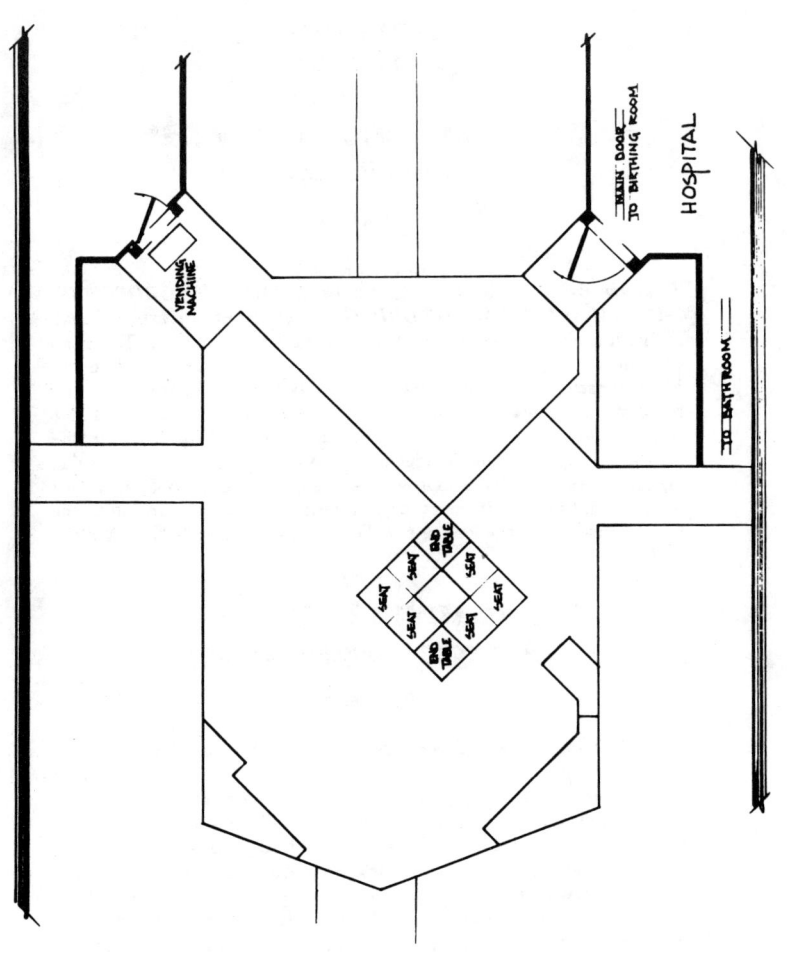

OTHER PUBLICATIONS FOR YOUR INTEREST

COASTAL DISTURBANCES
(Little Theatre- Comedy)

by TINA HOWE

3 male, 4 female

This new Broadway hit from the author of *PAINTING CHURCHES, MUSEUM,* and *THE ART OF DINING* is quite daring and experimental, in that it is *not* cynical or alienated about love and romance. This is an ensemble play about four generations of vacationers on a Massachusetts beach which focuses on a budding romance between a hunk of a lifeguard and a kooky young photographer. Structured as a series of vignettes taking place over the course of the summer, the play looks at love from all sides now. "A modern play about love that is, for once, actually about love--as opposed to sexual, social or marital politics . . . it generously illuminates the intimate landscape between men and women." --NY Times. "Enchanting."--New Yorker. #5755

APPROACHING ZANZIBAR
(Advanced Groups—Comedy)

by TINA HOWE

2 male, 4 female, 3 children --Various Ints. and Exts.

This new play by the author of *Painting Churches, Coastal Disturbances, Museum,* and *The Art of Dining* is about the cross-country journey of the Blossom family--Wallace and Charlotte and their two kids Turner and Pony--out west to visit Charlotte's aunt Olivia Childs in Taos, New Mexico. Aunt Olivia, a renowned environmental artist who creates enormous "sculptures" of hundreds of kites, is dying of cancer, and Charlotte wants to see her one last time. The family camps out along the way, having various adventures and meeting other relatives and strangers, until, eventually, they arrive in Taos, where Olivia is fading in and out of reality--or is she? Little Pony Blossom persuades the old lady to stand up and jump up and down on the bed, and we are left with final entrancing image of Aunt Olivia and Pony bouncing on the bed like a trampoline. Has a miracle occurred? "What pervades the shadow is Miss Howe's originality and purity of her dramatic imagination."--The New Yorker. #3140